CHAPTER VI

By

Roberto Beras

Roberto_Beras@hotmail.com

ISBN# 9780998867106

Eaton Literary Agency, Inc.
Post Office Box 49795
Sarasota, Florida 34230-6795
Federal Identification Number: 59-2370060

Representing: Roberto Beras

Chapter VI

ACKNOWLEDGEMENTS

I am extremely grateful to the following extraordinary people: Porfirio Mejia, for the selfless contribution of his time; and to my sister, Ana Cummins, and my son, Robertico, who so kindly gave me their support.

PROLOGUE

Roberto's work necessarily moves us to think deeply about it. It brings us to the metaphor of the constant struggle between good and evil; a struggle that is going on on Earth as it is in heaven, where supposedly only God, the angels and the blessed one inhabit.

The author, reflecting himself on the main character of his novel, tries to improve the strength of his faith while experiencing the hopelessness that a justice system lacking of a minimum sense of justice offers to him. The work focuses, in the most vivid way possible, on the vulnerability of being in a totally dehumanized society. A society, which has banished compassion from this world, to establish malignancy among fellow human beings.

Chapter VI, which title is not suggestive—although undoubtedly it is a story inherent to the author, to his own experience, where through the main character the author expresses his frustrations, but fatality never overwhelms him—is a novel that serves as a mirror and that in its reflection it gives us back the images, not only of the author, but of so many others, who, like him, suffer the pain of injustice.

Once into the book, we will begin to give value to its title because, a priori, it does not give us its meaning. The title does not create any expectation or suggest specific meanings, much less induce any conclusions. It is a kind of conceptual framework of the work because it is part of the context and is only seen from within. And at the end, we can clearly see that it really reveals the intention of the author, because the title itself, rather than a replacement by number, is an absence of title, which as such, is also full of meaning.

Chapter VI is a novel whose development quickly reveals its end and surprise, yet only surprises us in its part *in fini.* An extremely subliminal surprise, reserved for those who manage to discern the infinite desire of the author, and the harsh reality that the book also reflects. A surprise that demands a non-intellectual understanding of the work, but a sensible understanding of the core principles based on which we should live by.

Chapter VI is a very emotional novel which we will praise once we read it; where the author overcomes and breaks the shell to give us his story, exposing, more than his failure, his misfortune, in a crime quite different from his baseless accusation, but it is still a crime. He explains, with the simplicity of his language but with full knowledge of the legal issues and procedural violation involved, the violations of the most basic rights that all citizens of the world must enjoy. Violations suffered by a protagonist who was really him, but who were also Peter Limone, Enrico Tameleo, Louis Greco, and Joseph Salvati in the case Limone v. United States, 497 F. Supp. 2d 143 (D. MA 2007).

Chapter VI will also be read with the desire of those who have before their eyes the pages of a good work of suspense. At first glance it seems undeniable that Chapter VI was intended for the reader with some relation to unfair judicial processes, perhaps because of the almost indelible stigma with which society tries to reject or excludes from its circles those who, like the author, were unjustly prosecuted by the Justice

Department of the United States. However, the fate of the book is universal and can be enjoyed by all.

This novel, written while the author was in prison for an alleged act that not only he never committed, even worse, by an alleged act that is not even typified within the United States Code Service as a punishable offense, is a novel that enjoys an elaborated plot full of suspense and expectation and full of great emotions, despite an end that the same work constantly outlines.

Tony, the main character on whom the author discharges the responsibility of his own representation to carry out his project, after proving that he was wrongfully convicted for a crime he did not commit, in his first attempt to reintegrate himself into society, falls again. First, a victim of a destiny that seems to conspire against him, and second, victim of a new injustice, which becomes the leitmotiv of the novel.

With an unlimited imagination, Roberto combines the strength of his faith with the catharsis that he distills in his work through Tony and that without a doubt was the genesis of inspiration; a prodigious imagination that allows him to question God and the Holy Trinity without detracting from his manifest devotion, when he begins by showing his displeasure, in a jocular and hilarious way, with God and all the inhabitants of heaven, trying to communicate with a God who at that moment He had lost the gift of ubiquity and his omnipotence. Chapter VI describes the events in heaven with exaggerated mockery. Even so, it does not require a show of compunction, because that same hilarity dilutes until almost disappearing any sight of blasphemy and there is not even an indication of Tony reneging his faith or apostasy. Tony continues adhered to his faith and persists in talking with Jesus; he tries hard to speak out against injustices. And once he is successful in doing so, he denounces his injustices as part of a plan of Satan himself, embodied in the most powerful human on Earth, exclusively responsible for all the evils and injustices suffered by Tony, and with Tony, for practically the rest of humanity, with the exception of that powerful man's henchmen.

Chapter VI

The book brings us a comforting victory of good over evil. In Chapter VI, each element is in its place and each turn in the chain of events has a reason. The same God or the same destiny that allows the injustices against Tony, is the same God or the same destiny that reaches out his hand for his salvation, when an angel is incarnated in a prosecutor who decides to segregate himself from evil.

One definitively should read Chapter VI, not only to appreciate the potential of its powerful narrative, but more than anything else, to predict the future of the author when the doors, so unjustly and absurdly closed, are opened, to close again behind him with formidable rumble and forever.

Dr. Nelson Solano

CHAPTER ONE

As with every night, he struggled to get to sleep. He took a magazine from under the mattress and began reading, but after a few pages, he set it down. He took out photos of his children and studied them carefully. It was painful and wouldn't help him sleep, so he set those aside, too.

Finally, he took the Bible in his hands and read a chapter from it, falling asleep without realizing it.

It was 12:31 AM when the phone rang. Peter was still awake when his assistant transferred the call to him.

"Sir, I know it's very late, but I believe the call is important. It's from Earth. He said it's urgent, and he wants to speak with Jesus."

"From Earth?"

"Yes, Sir."

"What's his name?"

"I don't know, Sir. When I asked, he remained silent. What I can perceive, though, is that he's truly angry. There's venom in his voice."

Chapter VI

"Pass it on to me."

"Yes, Sir."

"It's late, Son. How can I help you? This is Peter."

"What difference is it if it's extremely late or very early? You guys are always there for us at any time, aren't you?" After a brief pause, the voice continued. "I want to talk to Jesus. Put him on the phone."

Peter immediately noticed the caller's anger. "Listen, Son. I sense anger in your tone. Could you explain what the problem is? That's the only way I can help you solve it. You know anger doesn't lead to anything good."

"Don't tell me that. Anger is common among you. Do you remember when Jesus entered the temple in Jerusalem and threw out all the people selling and buying? He overturned the tables of the money changers and destroyed the seats of those selling doves. He was filled with anger, so what's the difference between Him and me? We were made in His image and likeness, weren't we? Answer me!"

"Son, Jesus was very angry, because

usurers were using the Temple of His Father as a market."

"Oh, yeah. You know what? I'm angry, because here on Earth, they're marketing with the souls of the unfortunate and poor, and Jesus isn't doing anything. I want to talk to Him. I want to tell Him what I feel and to ask if He is causing the cruelty and injustice we live with here, or if it's the work of others, and He doesn't care. Or is it that He's so engaged with His Father's business, that He no longer has time for the unhappy people on Earth?"

"Son, in our celestial activities, which you call business, we have the daily task of protecting you in those moments of confusion."

"Well, then, carry out your tasks! Don't allow witnesses to give false testimony or become accomplices of the wicked, serving as witnesses in favor of injustice. Don't let the citizens of Earth be led by corrupt governments, bending down before what isn't fair. Don't allow evildoers to become our idols, and neither allow us to endorse their injustices. Don't allow them to use God's name to do evil, and if evil is committed, don't let them go without punishment.

"Bring the entire weight of the law upon those who commit murder. Don't let them live even one minute in freedom. Condemn those who take food from the hungry, who hide in darkness to strip us of our property, and don't let them walk down the street displaying the fruit of their crimes.

"Examine rigorously those who hurt families through lies. Once you do that, Peter, I'll believe you protect us and are taking care of us. Otherwise, save your words. You've left us in an abyss of anguish and pain, cruelty and injustice. You have given power and authority to the wicked. They govern us negligently, and you never examine what they do, much less investigate their intentions before granting them power.

"They don't observe the law with righteousness, nor do they act according to the will of Jesus, but you still protect them, while the unhappy and poor are being judged harshly by you and treated badly.

"Why do you treat us severely when they're the wicked ones? Answer me, Peter! Don't remain silent. Why don't you protect us from the wicked? You guys really don't know the suffering and misery we experience. Jesus doesn't know of the ten million children who die each year from hunger because of the corruption of the powerful. Answer me!"

"My Son, you're wrong. We don't protect the wicked. They will have much pain. The humble and poor have only to trust in God, and His love will cover them. You're a wonderful project of God's. He wants you to be happy, and He is vigilant, so the project is firm. He's looking at you from here and sees all that you're doing on Earth. Trust us, and God will protect you.

"Remember that God made a Covenant with you. He didn't just make it with your ancestors but with all who inhabit the Earth today. If this agreement is unfulfilled, God will exert His power and punish all those who violate it with fire. God was truly clear. He'll punish those who are called to give verdicts but do so with injustice. He'll punish whoever favors the weak and those who surrender to the powerful. The right thing is to live attached to justice. Don't take part in the acts of injustice nor keep hate in your heart. That will make you sick.

"Don't be complicit in the sin of liars. Only practice our laws, and God will protect you."

"I'm remarkably familiar with the content of the Covenant, but it seems that Jesus no longer cares if it's respected. Why doesn't He exercise His power? What's happening on Earth is the opposite of what you're telling me.

"The heartless and powerful humiliate us. We're subjected to torture with our families, condemned to death without any consideration, but you still protect them. They get drunk on expensive wine and leave traces of their joy everywhere. They have crushed men of honor who have no fortune. They have no compassion for our children and make a mockery of not only earthly justice but heavenly justice. The powerful start dreadful wars because of their ambition for power and money. They don't respect life. They stab us in the back. Everything in the world of the powerful and evil is done to create confusion, death, theft, deceit, bribery, adultery, and false oaths. They live in a world of injustice and envy.

They don't respect the dignity of other human beings.

"Peter, I'm convinced Jesus no longer cares about these things. Either that, or the suffering, injustice, and cruelty we're subjected to are unknown to Him. I insist on speaking with Him. Only He can clarify my doubts. Even the Virgin Mary hasn't wanted to discuss my complaints. All I hear is sadness in her voice when she evades my questions."

"Do something for me, Son. Call me in the morning, and I'll see what I can do to connect you with Jesus. What's your name?"

The call was cut off abruptly.

Peter immediately called his assistant. "Magdalene, sorry to wake you. Could you come to my office immediately?"

"Yes, Sir," she replied.

To Magdalene, it was obvious something unusual was happening. In all her years of service in the Heavenly Palace, no one ever woke her at 2:30 in the morning, much less so urgently.

She covered her delicate, beautiful body with a white cloak that had its borders sealed with brilliance. She knotted her hair and hurriedly slipped on white sandals before running down the hall toward Peter's office.

His office was a large, dark room lit by dozens of chandeliers, connected to a basement of the Palace, to which only security personnel, Peter, and Magdalene had access. Two heavenly agents were responsible for surveillance of the basement, while three others made sure that prisoners survived.

"Sit down Magdalene," Peter said.

"Thank you, Sir." She sat her frail body in one of the thirteen seats placed in an arc before Peter's desk, her face uneasy. "Is something serious happening, Sir?"

"I'm afraid so. Since God met Moses in the wildness of Sinai, there has been no further communication between Him and Earth, we have answered every terrestrial prayer as best we can, and they haven't suspected. Now, however, I'm afraid our project is in danger. Whoever made that last call is incredibly determined to speak with Jesus."

"Whoever? You don't know who he is?"

"Yes. When I asked for his name, the call was cut off. I don't know if he avoided my question or didn't hear me."

"I don't understand your concern, Sir, but if you don't pass the call to Jesus, our risk is eliminated."

"That wouldn't be prudent. We can't arouse any suspicion. In addition, he'd insist on talking to Jesus, even though I spent almost two hours talking to him. In addition, he's in constant communication with the old lady. She, in her kindness, will transfer the call to her Son despite the prohibition."

"What should we do, Sir?"

"The first thing is to take all these files to the basement and place them in a room alongside the prisoners' cells. They'll be safe there in case there's any investigation. No one will ever find them, just as no one has discovered our prisoners."

"Immediately, Sir."

"Call the five officials who are responsible for the custody and service in the basement to help carry these files downstairs."

Chapter VI

Peter's office was filled with golden boxes that served as files containing hundreds of memos generated internally in the Heavenly Palace. There was also every piece of correspondence generated in the Palace and sent to Earth. Within those files, there was also the fake memorandums that replaced the ones dictated by Jesus.

Thirty minutes later, with the help of the agents, Magdalene moved half of the gilded boxes and their contents to the basement. The prisoners were talking quietly to each other. They'd been held there for 2,000 years and had never seen Magdalene in that part of the Palace. They only met the agents who guarded them and a few servants, who provided two hot meals a day and blankets to protect the prisoners from the terrible cold. Her appearance triggered more conversation.

It was a mystery why she betrayed them and helped keep them locked up. She was once a faithful contributor and influential friend of Jesus'. The cells had twelve-foot-high by six-feet-wide walls covered in gold and a floor made of the finest stones. The roof arced overhead with holes to vent incense smoke. There was sufficient lighting to see who visited the basement. Powerful bronze bars prevented any of the prisoners from leaving, although they could see and speak with each other easily. All suspected something was happening, but it was impossible to know what.

On her way back to Peter's office, Magdalene felt nervous, and her face was filled with affliction. It was shocking to be close to those who had been faithful companions and collaborators for so many years. By her betrayal, they were buried in a cold basement, away from Jesus and His plans.

"Something wrong, Magdalene?" Peter asked, when she returned.

"No, Sir. I'm just a little tired. What's next, Sir?"

"I'm not sure how to proceed. Could you come up with something?"

"The first step is to identify that caller and to prevent him at all costs from communicating with Jesus."

Chapter VI

"I've been thinking about that. It's impossible to access the heavenly books that record the words and actions of humans. Those reports are extremely sensitive and can be obtained only when one is presented before Him."

"We should assign that task to our agents, so they can communicate with our representative on Earth. He has the means to obtain that information and should be able to identify the caller.

"Do it. Meanwhile, put our celestial informants on alert. We need to know Jesus' reaction if He should ever talk to the person who made that call."

"Ycs, Sir. I'll convene with our agents and informants immediately. They'll be alerted before any communication with Jesus occurs."

She summoned their agents and informants, who were immediately brought to Peter's office and told what happened.

"You've been faithful to our project and have followed my mandate," Peter said. "You have fulfilled my laws, and I thank you for that. However, as Magdalene just told you, our project is in danger. There's the possibility someone from Earth might converse with Jesus. I'm confident you know what that means."

The others murmured softly to each other.

"This danger can be eliminated if we act quickly and with great caution," Peter continued. "Our task is to locate who made that call and neutralize him. You know our representative on Earth. I want you to communicate with him immediately and ask for his help."

Peter's gaze went to his top agent, who understood that it was meant as a direct order. The top agent, a small man with a cold, calculating attitude, was in charge of the security of the Heavenly Palace and of preventing any human being from contacting Jesus. His face usually bore a strange expression, and he was easily distinguished by his moustache, which was shaved on both sides with a significant portion left in the middle. He came to the Heavenly Palace in recent years with the assistance and intervention of Peter's representative on Earth. The man had an extensive history of action, with the seal of evil on every chapter, which was enough to earn him the position of Peter's top agent.

"Sir, I'll use our satellite to send a message to our representative on Earth," the top agent said.

"I don't think that's a good idea. The celestial towers openly receive signals from satellites that contain the words and actions of humans. Those are archived in the book of God without being verified. However, satellite signals that come out are intercepted by the celestial towers and subjected to scrutiny. That's why, for the last two thousand years, we've sent messages through our agents. It's the only way those false memorandums arrive safely on Earth."

"That being so, Sir, a commission will immediately depart for Earth. Just to be clear, Sir, I will state what I understand to be an order. We will arrive on Earth, will locate our representative, and will request an investigation about the person who made the call. We will send you a report as soon as possible. Once we have possession of the information, we will return."

"Right, but it has to be before dawn. It's already 3:30 AM Earth time."

"Permission to leave, Sir?"

"Granted, but one more thing—ask our representative to provide us with a detailed report of everything that's been accomplished in the last sixty years."

Once outside Peter's office, the top agent outlined his plans. Many of his agents volunteered for the mission, but he said he would take care of it personally.

"Sir, I disagree with you," one agent said. "You haven't been to those areas or met our representative on Earth. On the other hand, I've been in communication with him for years and know the limits of his territory."

The top agent smiled, stroking his moustache. "I know our representative on Earth much better than you can imagine. I also know every corner on Earth. Unlike you, I come from there. As I said, I'll carry out this mission.

"You're to take care of this place and strictly monitor the situation in conjunction with our informants. Try to learn Jesus' plans, if He ever talks to this person. His call is expected at dawn, so be very careful. I'll leave immediately. I need three agents to accompany me."

He pointed with his index finger and chose three from the group, who welcomed the invitation.

"We leave now," the top agent said. "We'll use the time tunnel. We'll arrive a few minutes later, but it's much safer."

He was right. His background on Earth made him the most-qualified person to carry out the mission Peter assigned.

He initiated the first stage of his life on Earth when he was born on April 20, 1889, in Austria, Germany. As a child, he was a good student in elementary school, but, once he entered secondary school, he became less devoted to his studies. His father, a temperamental man, punished him constantly to the point where he physically abused him many times. Neither the abuse nor his father's punishment made him change. Instead of the professional man his father wanted him to become, he wanted to be an artist.

When his father died, he went to Vienna, the capital of Austria-Hungary, where he hoped to become an art student, but he failed the academy's admissions test twice. Despite that, he continued painting. With sales of his paintings and the pension he received after his mother's death in 1907, he lived comfortably during his stay in Vienna, where he considered himself a true artist.

Art was a talent he inherited from his mother, a country girl who, at the age of twenty-eight, contracted a marriage with a fifty-one-year-old customs officer. He was their only son, although he had several half-brothers from his father's previous and subsequent marriages.

Since he was a teenager, he became interested in politics and formed his own ideology. He admired the effectiveness of leadership and organization of the Democratic Party in Vienna. While growing up, he felt contempt for all foreigners living in what he called his nation. He constantly said, "No government would remain if we treat people of different nationalities with equality."

Chapter VI

In 1913, he moved back to Munich, Germany. The Austrian army called him to enlist, but he was later rejected due to his physical condition. When the First World War began in 1914, he volunteered for the German Army and was accepted.

He served bravely in the war, often taking part in the bloodiest battles. He was wounded in combat and was decorated twice for bravery, although Germany lost the war. When he was in the hospital, where he recovered from temporary blindness due to exposure to mustard gas in combat, he swore he would save Germany from any foreign threat.

His hatred grew when he learned of the sanctions imposed against Germany over the cost of the war, and his refusal to accept such authorities was great. He couldn't accept the fact that the current government signed a treaty that made Germany responsible for the war. The cost of such an acceptance were too great in his mind.

Once he recovered and left the hospital, he went to Munich and remained in the army until 1920. One year before resigning from the army, he began to participate in meetings of the Workers' Party.

He gained power within that party and later changed its name by adding the word Socialist. Eventually, that party's name became the Nazi Party. He immediately began calling for the government to renounce the existing treaty and asked all Germans to unite and form a single nation that refused the rights of all aliens.

He mobilized the masses, which earned him imprisonment for treason to his homeland. While in prison, he created his plan to conquer most of Europe and those territories lost in the First World War. He constantly blamed the Jews for all the evil on Earth and accused them of corrupting everything they touched.

After leaving prison, he became involved in politics full time and become a strong leader. During his campaigns, he used any possible means, including terror, to gain more power.

He immediately drew up plans to start World War Two. He wanted Germany to become the supreme power on Earth. During that war, he caused more death and destruction than any person or country before him in modern history. He told his soldiers to "have no compassion" and to "act brutally." He ordered tens of thousands of people executed for opposing his ideology. Hundreds of thousands more were put into prison. He persecuted the Jews in particular, killing more than six million of them. He also ordered the deaths of another five millions people who belonged to races he considered inferior. He soon came to conquer most of the territories he wanted, but his empire faded due to his self-centered errors. He rejected any recommendation from his commanders and had little respect for them.

This caused a progressive weakening of his armies to the point where his empire collapsed against an international coalition that fought his bloody politics. In 1945, he died a coward beside his lover. Both preferred to die by suicide than to respond to the holocaust they caused.

CHAPTER TWO

The trip to Earth took only seven minutes. Once on the ground, they went to the north side, to their representative and ally. They used public transportation, although they kept themselves invisible. Sometimes, however, they used physical appearances so they could question people about their destinations.

It was 4:00 AM when they arrived at the mansion of their ally. His mansion was painted white, with an enormous expansion on the west side that served as offices, followed by a single huge office that was carefully decorated. A huge, oval-shaped desktop sat in the center of that office, with seventeen chairs spaced around it and additional chairs behind those. Mahogany and sunlight made the room very attractive.

A large corridor connected to the white mansion and went up to the eastern part, where an office building stood. In the center of the roof was a beautiful flag of blue, red, and white, using a design made up of stars and stripes. At the front, a horseshoe-shaped structure served to give access to the interior.

The top agent and his men stopped in a building near the white mansion. It was as if the place brought an unexpected memory to the top agent, who entered the building carefully. Though the others didn't see it, his face reflected concern.

His fear was well-founded, because it was in that building that the decision was made to prosecute him for the Holocaust he caused. He toured the building from one end to the other. It was a large structure, with two huge conference rooms on the west side. The first one, in the west, looked modern and held 435 people, while the other was antiquely decorated and seemed abandoned.

In the center of the building was a large, round lounge. Following it to the east, he saw another structure that also looked abandoned. It was a huge office with the capacity for at least 100 seats. Three well-designed steps in front of the place provided access.

He toured the building from end-to-end. In the west end, he saw 100 people gathered, and he smiled in derision and satisfaction. The people inside discussed issues of war in the eastern part of Earth without reaching any agreement. He smiled to know that, even after his death, the Earth was still at war. The fact that his evil ideas had taken root was very satisfying.

He left the building to rejoin his men, who waited while watching the guards around the building.

"Anything new, Sir?" one asked.

"No. Let's continue."

They walked to the White House and moved unseen past the soldiers at the door, who stared beyond them. All had something in common—a piece of white lace left their chest and stretched to their ears above their suits and ties.

The agents walked to the west side of the building and stood in the enormous oval office, carefully decorated with a Christmas tree loaded with ornaments. A beautiful flag stood near the main doorway, and expensive paintings adorned the walls with a few credenzas embedded in them. The floor was made of cream and brown marble with an embossed design.

Chapter VI

In the center of the room, a large mahogany writing desk sat with black leather armchair. Additional seats were placed in front of the desk. Only one person was present when the top agent entered. He became visible immediately and gave his Earthly ally a hug. Both were excited to meet again.

"Adolf, it's a real pleasure to see you," the man said. "What's this visit about?"

"It's a pleasure for me, too, Louis. I'll explain immediately. Our project is in danger."

"Well, it seems that once again you need my help. I still remember the day when I met you in the bunker. The truth is, I thought you wouldn't have the courage for suicide, much less be able to persuade your wife to do it, too. By the way, how is she? Have you seen her?"

"Not yet. My people tell me they've seen her in the corridors of the building in front of the Heavenly Palace. She's there often, but I haven't had the joy of seeing her. I regret very much that it's been impossible to bring her to the Palace with us."

"Yeah, I know, and I understand, my

friend." He knew that it was a risk to try to get her into the Palace. "I'm sure she'll run into your arms when you meet, which will make identifying you two much easier. By the way, how is our friend, Herod, doing?"

"He's very worried right now. You know he won't give up despite the danger. What he has is much more than an obsession. He's frustrated, because he failed to kill Jesus when he was a child, but he believes he can do it now that he's so close to Him. He'll support your plans as long as his are carried out."

"Nobody has suspected the plagiarism?"

"Not yet. That's part of my job, you know, to protect your identity and, above all, mine. I've been highly effective, as were the previous security chiefs. Actually, it's not been that difficult due to the strong resemblance between them."

"It seems you've been especially useful to us. It was worth the risk to falsify your identity. Of course, we must thank Magdalene for your acceptance into the Heavenly Palace. I assume she knows who you are, doesn't she?"

Chapter VI

"True, and I really appreciate your help. I feel much better being there."

"Tell me what the threat to our project is."

"Our friend received a call from here around the middle of the night. Whoever called insisted on speaking with Jesus. He was filled with anger and frustration and demanded answers to the damage you're causing here. He believes Jesus is doing it, and he wants an explanation.

"As you know, if he should ever speak with Jesus, Jesus would learn about the real events on Earth and will know our reports are false. What's worse, he would discover the plagiarism, and our project would be neutralized."

"I don't understand the gravity of this matter. Why not refuse to transfer the call?"

"That's been considered, but whoever called is also in contact with old Mary. Our friend believes that she would transfer the call to Jesus if the man asked hard enough."

"How was this person about to communicate with Mary? I thought all our communications were secure."

"They aren't that safe, Louis. In recent

years, we've found signs that our system is more vulnerable than we knew. For over 2,000 years, people have been limited to using only prayer, which our satellites can capture. Recently, there have been increasing attempts to communicate through direct waves. We have successfully transferred those to our friend and his team, and they handled them so far."

"I understand. I always suspected the existence of exchanges of information between terrestrial and Martian agencies. Only the Martians have that kind of technology."

"Our friend asks that you open an investigation and find who's been calling. Once you've prepared a report, hand it to me and wait for his recommendations. In addition, our friend begs you to inform him how much the project has advanced on Earth in the last sixty years."

"The investigation will take an hour. I'll get my assistants started immediately. I'll also order a complete report of my efforts here. What was the name of the caller?"

"We don't know yet."

"That will take a little more research, but

don't worry. We'll get you the information in time. I'll be back."

The top agent settled himself in a comfortable chair in the Oval Office. His agents remained standing, although they looked at the details in the beautifully decorated office.

Louis returned quickly. "I've given the instructions, my friend. The research has begun."

"As I informed you, our friend also wants a report on the progress of our project. We don't know much about the last few years."

"That's true. Due to excessive work, I haven't been able to keep you informed. I assure you I'm still steadfast in our project. We'll achieve our goal. I'll be the king of the universe, with a stranglehold on all this. Most importantly, Jesus will be blamed for all the cruelties and injustices I've caused. People will hate Him and worship me."

"You have concrete plans to achieve this?"

"Sure. The last few years have been some very hard work. I've been concentrating on eliminating ninety percent of the inhabitants of

Earth. In some way or another, all of them identify with Jesus, so that makes them a danger to us. The other ten percent follow us and support the project."

"You're talking about ninety percent of the inhabitants of Earth? That doesn't sound realistic. How will you achieve something like that?"

"I know it sounds unreal, but believe me, I'll make it happen. The work routines and the effort of people to make money every day are my best allies. They never stop to think how to implement methods to keep them healthy. This, together with a greedy media, facilitates my work."

"I still don't understand. Explain it some more."

"Of course, my friend. Within a few years, one-third of the world's population will suffer from one of my most-effective weapons—cancer. Just in this region of the Earth, with a population of just over 300 million, 140 million of those will soon be suffering. Currently, I'm causing the deaths of at least 600,000 a year with only that disease."

Chapter VI

"How is it possible you're causing something like this? How can they get the disease without realizing its cause?"

"As I told you, my friend, Adolf, they're only trying to make fortunes and obtain material goods. They buy all the crap they see announced in the media, and through them, I introduce food products that cause cancer when eaten in excess. Of course, my faithful friends on Earth have contributed a lot to my project. They created chains of fast-food restaurants, where all those products are distributed. Just one of those companies, with branches in every corner of Earth, reported sales of over $15 billion every year.

"Of course, my friends benefit economically. They live in abundance. McDonald's Corporation has accumulated earnings of over $16 billion. This, in conjunction with Burger King, Kentucky Fried Chicken, Denny's, and others, make attaining my goals easy by distributing cancer effectively. That excludes the effects of obesity, which adds about 300,000 deaths a year."

"If I remember correctly, before my last

departure from Earth, one medicinal formula that eradicates cancer was already being processed and just needed approval to be used."

"That's right. It's called Carcomax. In less than three months, it eliminates cancer completely, but the greed and indifference of government officials is more powerful than any effort made to get this medication to the market.

"In exchange for juicy dollar amounts, these officials eliminate any possibility that the medicine will ever be approved. All the members of the owner's family from the labs that discovered the formula died mysteriously. It's rumored that certain interest groups like the Medical Association, the Hospitals Corporation, and the Bar Association, along with clandestine government groups, have concentrated their efforts to ensure the drug is never approved, even if it costs the lives of those who would produce the drug. That eliminates any possibility of getting the drug into the market. The formula is still there. It's under guard at a university center in a northern state called Massachusetts."

"Why has this university failed to gain

approval?"

"Fear of disappearing like all the others who discovered the drug."

"Now I understand. This helps our plans."

"Yeah, Adolf. I also started deploying one of the most-powerful viruses we've created so far."

"Don't tell me you've started distributing MECOSA?"

"Not yet. That's my secret weapon. I'll use it at the end to eliminate anyone left alive."

MECOSA, one of the most-powerful, destructive viruses ever created by their group, was a method of freezing the blood. The letters stood for *Método de Congelación Sanguínea.* Even a microscopic portion was enough to cause a heart attack in seconds.

"What's being distributed now is HIV, the virus that causes acquired immune deficiency syndrome. Believe me, even though my plan to scare people enough to refrain from reproducing failed, the effects have been the same. Despite the huge amounts of money I've spent trying to educate them about HIV, the contagion has spread rapidly."

"Why spend time educating them so they won't be infected? Are you interested in their health?"

"Come on. Their health doesn't matter to me. I just want them to fear the HIV virus and not multiply. It's a way to slow population growth, so there won't be as many of them to deal with when I eliminate them all. They'll eliminate themselves while my plan reaches its final stage.

"Just from HIV alone over 10 million people die each year. If we add those numbers to the deaths caused by cancer and things like heart disease, alcohol, hunger, and suicidal depression, the mortality rate will quickly exceed the birth rate. Humans will start disappearing."

"You mentioned HIV. Isn't that the virus that causes AIDS?"

"Yes."

"But they've had the cure for that for years. I remember enemy troops released this virus along with mustard gas to neutralize us during the battles of the First World War. The effects of the virus and mustard gas sent me to the hospital for a long time. I almost went blind because of it.

I vomited, had diarrhea, fever, and terrible headaches. Luckily, I was injected when the vaccine was discovered and made a complete recovery."

"I know. The cure has always existed, but what happens with this virus is the same thing that happened to the secret formula to cure cancer. The government's interest groups kept the drug secret, especially when they realized that the virus attacked mostly the minority classes, not the elite. They wanted to keep the cure secret and use the virus as a weapon of mass destruction for enemy countries.

"When one of their own people is infected, he recovers miraculously, but the answer is he ingests a small amount of the secret drug. They're the only ones who have it."

"Humans haven't changed at all. Has it been difficult to manage this alone? When you acquired so much influence with humans, was your identity never discovered?"

"The truth is, it hasn't been easy. In the beginning, I wasn't sure how to carry out my plans. I spent many years wasting my time.

Finally, I did what Jesus did and acted like them, lived with them, thought like them, and adopted their appearance. That was the start of my plan, which is finally producing results. The plan just needed to be perfected.

"I started by coming from a human womb, from which I emerged as a small creature. I had to look authentic. I chose a respected, influential marriage in the upper echelons of society. In the beginning, it was difficult. Their integrity, principles, and values are totally opposed to my crazy way of promoting evil, but what could I do? I needed a couple with influence.

"I came to Earth and assumed a human form, having a normal childhood and adolescence. I completed my education as expected for a son of a worthy, respected society family. As an adult, I slowly infiltrated the upper levels, learning to play politics, because that was the game that would enable me to accomplish my plans. Getting into politics was easy. My parents were already in politics and had leadership and power.

"I immediately was elected as the governor of an important state in the western part of this country. There I learned the game of politics completely and confirmed what I thought—it was the game I had to play to accomplish my plans.

"While I learned, though, I continued to practice iniquity. I murdered more people as a governor than all the governors who preceded me combined! I used my position to make a fortune and deal easily with my environment. Then I used that fortune, along with the influence of my friends and parents, to reach my current position, the president of the most-powerful nation on Earth.

"Believe me, it wasn't easy. Everything had to look real. The process these people use to choose their primary official is by a majority of electoral votes after the people cast individual ballots. That wasn't favorable for me. I needed help from certain allies, all of whom responded quickly to give me the presidency.

"Do you know who represented me in that process? It was a direct descendant of Herod who remained incognito on Earth for many years. Of course, I had to return the favor and appoint him as Chief Justice of the Supreme Court with the discretion to hear cases he preferred.

"After my appointment, my plans were implemented effectively. It's been difficult to keep my identity hidden. There are times when my true identity comes out in a spontaneous way, which sometimes amazes me. There have been a few occasions when people have suspected who I am, but I managed to keep them confused.

"There was one time, however, when I almost lost control. It was during a meeting of all the presidents of Earth, when each one had the chance to address the audience. When it was my turn, I was so filled with energy, the smell of sulfur from my body escaped and flooded the podium. One president noticed the smell and discovered my identity. He immediately told the others and the rest of the world via the media coverage of the event.

"I still remember his words. 'The devil was here yesterday. I can still smell the aroma of sulfur in the area.' I spent a fortune paying my media allies to stop broadcasting his words. Of course, I injected cancer into him, and he will die soon. Aside from that time, everything has gone perfectly. I have all the pieces in place and am waiting for the right moment."

"What do you mean by that?"

"I intend to eliminate all the inhabitants of Earth. I want to create a world where I'm the one who's being worship as they worship Jesus now. He will be hated when I write the chapters of that story. My evil deeds will be attributed to Him, while His virtues will become mine. I'll get credit for all the good deeds Jesus did on Earth.

"I will destroy the world within minutes. Then my kingdom will be accepted as easily as people accepted the idea that Judas betrayed Christ, exonerating John from his betrayal."

"You think nobody knows it was John who betrayed Jesus, convincing him to admit he was the Son of God? We obtained specific information at the Heavenly Palace that it was John who betrayed Him. High Priest Caiaphas was the one who asked John to convince Jesus to admit he was the Son of God, and He did."

"At least no one questions it today. Of course, John was always on our side."

"How will you destroy the world?"

"I've already built the most-powerful bomb that ever existed. It's been tested. The results were amazing."

He meant a bomb made of ammonium nitrate fertilizer that was made in one of Earth's largest laboratories, known as Area 51. The bomb was tested at the bottom of the Pacific and Indian Oceans off the Indonesian coast, using only a tenth of its potential power. The explosion created a huge crater at the bottom of the ocean, causing a magnitude-nine earthquake and killing over 290,000 people. Detonating one of those bombs at its maximum capacity would cause a magnitude-ninety earthquake. The resulting tsunami would kill all but a few who lived well above sea level.

"This time," Louis said, "they'll believe there was another flood, as they believe what happened the last time."

"You really have all the pieces in place. Just out of curiosity, why'd you decide to try the bomb in that area and not close to the Vatican? Your real enemies would have died, and our current challenge would be far less risky."

Chapter VI

"One thing I've learned, my friend, is to be calculating. I performed that test in no man's land. Only the unhappy and needy of Earth live there, so events in that location don't matter to the powerful. If I detonated the bomb near the Vatican, in less than three hours countries like Britain and France would have discovered the cause of the tsunami. Since no one cares about that part of the Pacific, my secret will never be discovered."

"You're a genius. We should detonate that bomb immediately and distribute the MECOSA through the restaurants of your friends."

"Not yet, my friend. This plan has two stages, and you aren't ready for the second one, which requires taking control of the Heavenly Palace and taking Jesus prisoner, along with His army of angels and archangels."

"Certainly. I forgot that part."

CHAPTER THREE

Louis' assistants made inquiries to determine who called Peter. They went to the city that held the main office of the nation's bureau of investigation, identified by the acronym FBI.

Once there, they told the director their purpose. Their orders were issued by the Chief Executive Officer of that nation, but there was a problem. No one had a clue how to locate whoever made the call.

The director of the FBI was alarmed by the urgency attached to locating the person and by the lack of information he could offer.

"A drastic change in procedures must be established," he declared. "The last eight years have been frustrating ones for this office. Our work schedules and agendas have been subject to constant change due to the personal requests of your superiors. We've consumed more time chasing political enemies of your superiors than pursuing the enemies of this nation and the world. We've spent valuable time trying to convince the world of something that isn't real rather than being allowed to make the truth available."

Chapter VI

"Ben," Mrs. Rice said, "I'm only a messenger. I understand your frustration, but I assure you you'll be given time to express these things to Louis. Just give me the available information, and I'll see what I can do."

"We'll start immediately. Do you have the person's name?"

"Not yet."

"What's the record of the call?"

"All we have is the time. It was last night at 12:31 AM, and the call lasted approximately two hours."

"That shouldn't be too difficult to find. Such calls to the Heavenly Palace aren't common. Wait a moment."

The director left the office, abandoning Mrs. Rice and her companion, who seemed to be her bodyguard. She watched impatiently, as the director walked away.

Once he reached a huge room with large computer monitors on the walls, he delivered his request to one of the workers. He wore glasses with thick lenses that were attached to a blue cord around his neck. He must have weighed at least 400 pounds, and he moved from side-to-side with very slow steps, as if he were an old man, though he looked barely twenty-five. His white lab coat was identical to those the others in the room wore, but he wore a white helmet. The rest of the technicians wore gray ones.

The thick-spectacled young man waddled to a small office. It would take only a few seconds to identify the call and who placed it.

He fed the information into one of the larger computers in his office and immediately had a list of the calls made to the Heavenly Palace. It was easy to place the call that went to Peter. Only one such call was identified.

The manager captured the caller's voice and initiated a search using a range of one to three hours to capture recordings of the calls using a system known as Global Positioning System Recording, which had been secretly and illegally installed by Louis' government to constantly monitor everyone.

After fifty-four seconds passed, the computer's red button, labeled *REC*, was automatically activated, and a voice became audible. Once the voice was captured, it had to be identified. Although that might seem like a difficult task, the spectacled young man surprised himself by quickly identifying the person.

The computer used a system like a fingerprint detector, which instead identified voice prints. Once he entered the voice into the system, he gained access to that man's personal data. Thousands of such recordings already existed, originating from the same place.

He quickly accessed the numbers where those recorded calls originated and found they came from a man named Tony, a prisoner in a jail run by Louis and his accomplices. Who Tony was, however, didn't have a clear answer.

The young man quickly passed the information to the director, who returned to his office and told Mrs. Rice, who waited impatiently.

"We've made significant progress on this," the director said, "but we need additional time to obtain all information pertaining to this person."

Mrs. Rice glared at him. "You have three hours to complete your investigation."

"As soon as the report is finished, I'll bring

it to you personally."

She left, and the director launched an investigation. Louis' Bureau of Intelligence maintained a database of the activities of everyone on Earth who accessed the computer's system. It tracked every item, including phones, computers, pagers, credit cards, cars with digital radios, anyone boarding a train, and even electronic appliances used in the home, including children's games.

In one hour, Tony's entire life story was on its way to the White House. All were surprised when Ben walked in and placed a folder of Tony's history on Louis' desktop. Mrs. Rice was also in the room, though the top agent and his assistants remained invisible to Ben or Mrs. Rice.

"Thank you very much, Ben," Louis said. "Thank you, Mrs. Rice. I'll call you again if I need you."

CHAPTER FOUR

Once Ben and Rice left Louis' office, Adolf and his agents became visible.

"Let's read this immediately," Louis said.

Tony was one of the 65,000,000 people involved in the U.S. justice system. His lawyer recently published an article in a national newspaper that stated Tony was serving a prison sentence because of the corrupt conduct of officers of the U.S. government. His lawyer stated that those who allegedly performed their duties based on the U.S. Constitution were acting outrageously. She wanted to know which Constitution those corrupt officers referred to and which Congress they followed. She said it was difficult to understand how right and wrong could mean something different to the prosecutors, judges, and justice system officers involved in her case. Their actions had sunk so far that despite the country sinking into a deep economic crisis due to the war on terrorism, they were creating even more terror. Officials in the nation were doing nothing to prevent the officers from acting outrageously. If society didn't respond quickly, the nation's image would be damaged forever.

Tony Parker was the subject of an undercover investigation initiated by the El Dorado Task Force. His attorney described that group as a criminal gang formed by personnel from the U.S. Customs Department, agents from the IRS, and members of the New York City Police Department, formed in response to special interest groups with the clear objective of serving leading companies in the money-transfer industry, including Western Union and Money Gram. The El Dorado Task Force began Operation With Drill to investigate money-transmitting companies owned by people of ethnic backgrounds.

They also created the Geographical Targeting Order (GTO), following the order given by the Secretary of the Treasury to select and investigate companies specifically serving Dominican and Colombian communities in New York. They followed all the money being sent to the Dominican Republic and Colombia and added their own numbers to the total being generated by the hardworking ethnic communities in New York City.

Chapter VI

It seemed inconceivable that while Western Union and Money Gram had 97% of the market in money transfers, the task force investigated only the small businesses run by Dominicans and Colombians that took care of the remaining 3%.

After a long investigation, along with $400,000 paid to an informant named Julio Luna, who committed perjury in the U.S. District Court for the Southern District of New York in the case of *Narciso Ortis v. United States* (95-Cr-91 RJW), the government was unable to obtain any evidence that linked Tony with any illegal activity. Even without evidence, the government falsely accused him of violating the money laundering laws of the country. He was arrested by Federal agents and brought to trial before a jury.

Repeated violations of Tony's constitutional rights included; $400,000 paid to a corrupt informant who was never present in court to face Tony despite the claim he could offer evidence; the false testimony of Hendrix Tavares, an informant for the U.S. government after being found guilty in the Southern District of New York for money laundering; the government altering recorded conversations where Tony allegedly participated; secretly including in the jury a police officer from the City of New York; false testimony of a U.S. Secret Service agent who spoke about an analysis she never made; not allowing Tony to present any witnesses in his defense; defense counsel preventing Tony from testifying due to the fact that the judge presiding over the case alleged she was very ill and wanted to finish the trial as quickly as possible; and Charles A. Ross from the firm Brafman and Ross offering an ineffective representation of the criminal case.

In the end, the jury found Tony guilty of the allegations made against him.

CHAPTER FIVE

Like many prisoners in the U.S. justice system, Tony realized how ineffective his lawyer was after he lost the trial. He contacted other lawyers and visited the law library of the institution where he was imprisoned, spending at least ten hours a day with legal texts to familiarize himself with the law. His family supported him financially and emotionally during this process.

Hiring another lawyer, he used money from his wife and his children's school fund to pay him. He promised Tony he would have dinner with him and his family on the day of his sentencing. He felt certain the case would be overturned. At the very least, Tony would have the opportunity for a new trial, because there was insufficient evidence of his guilt and new evidence had been obtained during the investigation.

Tony contacted his family and gave them the good news. On the specified day, Tony and his family and friends were in the courthouse. All were disappointed when the judge sentenced Tony to 292 months in a federal prison over 600 miles from his home.

His lawyer continued making promises to Tony about the possibility of an appeal. Later, the lawyer refused Tony's phone calls.

Tony prepared himself by studying to become a paralegal, so he could contribute more to his case. The Court of Appeals set a date for his appeal brief to be submitted, accompanied by the respective arguments. However, his lawyer failed to submit the appeal on time. When he finally submitted the documents, he didn't include the legal arguments Tony told him to use. Those would have proven a clear violation of the law, so Tony would have been released.

The Court of Appeals denied Tony's appeal. After communicating with his lawyer, Tony realized the man hadn't studied his case and did much less research than he promised. Tony asked him certain questions about the case over facts that were on record, and the lawyer had no idea what he was talking about.

Tony fired his lawyer.

CHAPTER SIX

Tony was alone, facing an exceedingly difficult time due to his circumstances, but he nonetheless made a smart decision.

After completing a complicated process and despite his being in prison, Tony was able to register with a school of paralegals from Ashworth University to begin his studies. He studied in the law library every day, as he had since he entered prison.

Four years passed. Tony acquired his certificate in paralegal studies with a specialty in civil litigation. After he finished that arduous task, he felt ready to deal with the unfair justice system in the U.S.

As a paralegal, he managed to reopen his case and returned to court through a *habeas corpus* petition. The U.S. District Court for the Southern District of New York granted him a hearing where he would have the opportunity he never had before, to cross examine Hendrix Tavares, the main government witness, who was an informant willing to lie in exchange for certain concessions promised by corrupt police officers and an irresponsible prosecutor. Tony would also have his version of the facts heard by the judge.

The hearing began at ten o'clock. The courtroom was full of people, including Tony's family and friends. Court reporters, a secretary, and another staff member were present as well. A group of young law students was there to observe. The prosecutor was also there, accompanied by the police officers who participated in the investigation of the case.

The temperature in the room was barely 40 degrees Fahrenheit, yet Tony was sweating, and his hands shook. He never expected to face such a huge responsibility, where his life and that of his family depended on him. He stood before a judge, ready to fight for his life and his family's.

"Mr. Parker, are you ready to proceed?" the judge asked.

"Yes, Your Honor. The petitioner requests that the government informant, Hendrix Tavares, be called as a witness."

The prosecutor stood and objected. He was a young man just out of law school who began his legal career as a secretary. After a few months in that position, he became a federal prosecutor. Tony assumed the man's parents helped. His name was Edward Soliman, a short Caucasian man who wore thick glasses, a blue suit, with a white shirt and red tie.

"Your Honor," Soliman said, "as I explained in the motion in opposition to the defendant's request, I informed that Court that I am categorically opposed to this request."

Tony had submitted a motion to the Court not only requiring a hearing but also that the informant, Hendrix Tavares, should be present for questioning. The government wrote a memorandum opposing the request, but the Court granted the audience without taking a position concerning the witness. The Court stated that Tony would first have the opportunity to demonstrate to the Court sufficient reasons why Hendrix Tavares had to be present. The government would also have the opportunity to demonstrate why it wasn't necessary to present Hendrix to the court.

"Your Honor," Tony said, "as I specified in my petition, I will obtain overwhelming evidence by questioning the informant, Hendrix Tavares. He was the principal witness for the government against me in the trial, and I believe due to the inefficiency of the lawyer representing me during my trial, the informant, Tavares, wasn't properly questioned. I understand that is of great interest to this Court to resolve this case and that justice should prevail. I suggest, Your Honor, that the Court won't be in a position to do justice without the presence of the informant, Hendrix Tavares, and without the opportunity for me to question him."

"Does the government have anything to add?" the judge asked.

"Yes, Your Honor. In addition to the different reasons contained in the memorandum against the defendant, it is our position that, at this point, almost ten years after the trial, the memory of the witness Tavares could be affected."

"Your Honor," Tony said, "this case is a product of an old investigation and trial that took place quite some time ago. Many years passed before the trial began, and, according to the testimony of the informant, Hendrix Tavares, he recalled the facts quite well. I suggest that the informant Hendrix Tavares has shown he has a good memory."

The judge smiled.

"The government's suggestion is pure speculation, Your Honor, and should be denied," Tony added.

"OK. Enough. This session is ended until tomorrow at ten o'clock AM. The government will have to produce the witness."

Tony asked the officers who accompanied him to allow him to speak with his wife and children, so he could explain what happened. The officers nodded.

He returned to his cell. What happened in the court wasn't what he was waiting for, but it hadn't been the opposite, either. He was satisfied for having won a small battle against the government. However, he faced a very difficult task. He had to demonstrate, through interrogation of the informant, that Tavares lied during the trial.

He needed to rest. He would be awakened at 4:00 AM by a correctional officer for the next day's court appearance.

"All rise, Please," the secretary said. "The Court enters in session today. Judge Laxy will preside over the case *United States v. Tony Parker.*"

The government engineered the situation, so a judge of its pretence was assigned to the case.

"Mr. Parker, are you ready to proceed?" the judge asked.

"Yes, Your Honor. The petition calls the Government's informant, Hendrix Tavares, as a witness."

The clerk of the court took the witness' oath. Tony had many questions for the man. Although he prepared for a long time for that moment, his nervousness was obvious, and he found it difficult to begin.

"Good morning, Hendrix," he said. "I think it's unnecessary to introduce myself. We've known each other a long time, right?"

"Yes."

"Mr. Tavares, you offered very extensive testimony during the trial against me. You were here in this same courtroom offering your testimony for about three days. The Government asked you many questions, which you answered. You're probably familiar with these questions, true?"

"Yes, I answered many questions. Yes, I'm familiar with those questions."

"Today I'll ask you almost the same questions you answered before. Mr. Tavares, you testified during the trial that you had no participation in the money-laundering conspiracy the Government charged you with."

"Correct."

"Was it your testimony that Tony Parker was the one running those illegal activities, and that you knew nothing about that?"

"Yes."

"You described every step of the conspiracy and told the jury how it worked and where it took place. You explained who was involved, who was in charge, who was the leader, how the money was received, how he received the money, and those who were drug traffickers. You named each person who was allegedly involved in the conspiracy. You also explained to the jury the way in which the money was structured to evade government reports. Do you remember those questions, Mr. Tavares?"

"Yes."

"Now, Mr. Tavares, did you ever talk to Tony about the conspiracy and how it worked?"

"No."

"Did you speak with someone else about the conspiracy?"

"No."

"You never had conversations with anyone about what the conspiracy at the company Dinero Express was about?"

"Never."

"OK. Let me ask you this, Mr. Tavares. You pleaded guilty to money laundering in front of Judge Markison in this Court?"

"Yes."

"You pled guilty based on a cooperation agreement with the Government, right?"

"Yes."

"Your Honor," Soliman said, "I suggest the defendant should ask his question."

Chapter VI

"Mr. Parker," the judge said, "I suggest you state your question."

"Mr. Tavares, if you weren't involved in the conspiracy, if you didn't have any communication with any member in the conspiracy about how it worked, how can you explain so confidently to the jury how the conspiracy was carried out? How could you explain that you knew all the traffickers, the money they handled, who participated, and how it worked? Can you explain that to the court, Mr. Tavares?"

"Well...well...."

"Why did you plead guilty if you knew nothing about the conspiracy?"

"You know, well.... Well, you know...."

"Your Honor," Soliman said quickly, "we call for a recess."

"Answer the question, Mr. Tavares," the judge said.

"My lawyer told me.... You know...." Tavares kept looking at the prosecutor, as if waiting for his help. Tavares' nervousness was obvious.

"Don't look at the government's table," Tony

said. "Answer the question. If you had nothing to do with the conspiracy, how did you know so much about how it was run?"

"I spoke with.... He said...."

"No, Sir," Tony said. "You said a moment ago that you had no conversation with anyone who had anything to do with the conspiracy. How did you know about the conspiracy?"

"They told me.... They asked me to lie and accuse you."

"Who are they?"

"The pros. He told me...."

"Your Honor, we call for a recess!" Soliman said.

"Answer the question, Mr. Tavares," the judge said.

"I really need to talk to the government," Tavares said.

"We're waiting for an answer, Your Honor," Tony said.

There was a short silence. Everyone waited anxiously for the witness to answer, but he refused.

"I see you aren't able to answer these

questions, Mr. Tavares," Tony said, "so I'll ask you other questions. Many people were mentioned during the trial. I'll repeat them now. They were Tavares, Juan Carlos, Janet, Ivet, Aridio, Joselin, Madelin, Alberto, Liriano, Tito, Enna, Charo, Rafael, and Louis. According to your testimony, all those people were involved in the conspiracy, right?"

"Yes."

"They are all members of your family, correct?"

"Yes."

"I have no more questions, Your Honor. However, I'd like to point out to the Court that according to the testimony of the witness here today, it's obvious that he lied throughout this process. I suggest there is no one in this courtroom who doubts that the witness lied. I ask the Court that this case be dismissed, and the witness be accused of committing perjury. It's extremely likely that if my lawyer performed a proper cross-examination, the jury would have found me innocent of the charges. The petitioner rests, Your Honor."

"Does the government have anything to add?"

"Yes, Your Honor," Soliman said. "The government leaves to the Court any determination in relation to this hearing. The government rests, Your Honor."

"The court orders that the case be immediately dismissed, and Mr. Parker released from prison. With respect to the witness, the Court finds that he committed perjury. Therefore, the Court instructs the government to proceed according to the law. The witness has rights."

Manipulating the system didn't serve the government that time, because the judge decided in Tony's favor.

"Mr. Tavares," Soliman began, "you are under arrest and have the right to remain silent...."

Hendrix Tavares returned to the Court ten months later as a witness against the police officers who led the investigation. The agent in charge and his assistants were charged with interfering with a government investigation and tampering with evidence against Tony, and with witness tampering.

CHAPTER SEVEN

Tony returned to prison for one day. The judge who presided over the case ordered him to return to comply with the formalities of the Bureau of Prisons. He was released the following day.

Once out of the place where he spent eleven years of his life, he felt a strange sense of anxiety, as if looking back risked his freedom. Still, he studied the facilities and pictured every detail in his mind, as he walked to the parking area where the prison officer waited to transport him to the Cleveland, Ohio airport. His flight was scheduled to depart at 11:55 AM and to arrive at Kennedy Airport in New York at 2:15 PM.

While driving, the female officer showed her support by saying, “I’m glad you made it happen, Tony. Good luck. I know you’re a good person. You showed me the same respect as you gave to the team in our unit.”

With tears in his eyes, Tony said, “I’ll miss you.”

She touched his left hand. “I know you will.”

Chapter VI

When she pulled up at exit door number 23 for American Airlines, she added, "I'll miss you, too." She touched his hand once more. For a moment, they looked into each other's eyes, as if an unknown feeling were awakening in them.

He got out and said good-bye. Tony would miss her. She was a beautiful woman of twenty-five, with golden skin and beautiful hair that fell to her shoulders. Her gorgeous blue eyes were adorned with golden lashes.

She was a slender woman of five-feet-six who smiled often, showing her white teeth and wet lips, but her outer beauty was surpassed by her inner beauty. She could accept all who felt rejected, able to understand those who weren't understood. She could smile at someone in the midst of sadness, able to make someone feel free for a moment even when in prison.

She was a special person who gave Tony reasons to smile when he felt unable to deal with his pain.

CHAPTER EIGHT

Flight 0407 had no delays and took off at 12:06 PM. The flight attendants announced their destination, as Tony sat in seat 19B and finally realized he was free.

His thoughts were interrupted when a sexy woman of thirty sat in the seat beside him. The beautiful woman looked into his eyes, as if waiting for a formal introduction.

Finally, he said, “Hello. My name’s Tony.”

“A pleasure. My name’s Roanne. I hope we have a pleasant trip.”

“I hope so, too. Are you from New York?”

“Yes. I’m going back after a business trip. I was attending public hearings in Cleveland. My boss thought it was worth the time to participate, because the topic is one that has high priority in our organization—justice.”

“Did you say justice?”

“Yes. Our organization is called the Innocence Project. We’re focused on the number of people in prison who are innocent of the crimes they were charged with, particularly those who face the death penalty. In the last ten years, we have gained the freedom of 292 prisoners when DNA evidence showed they were innocent.

"Even with those results, we're struggling to continue the project, because the indifference to the problem within the justice system is increasingly apparent. Inexplicably, and at the request of government lawyers, the courts have begun denying us permission to reexamine evidence of cases of other prisoners who are potentially innocent."

There was a moment of silence, as if Tony wasn't paying attention to her, then he said, "I know what you guys do."

She opened her briefcase and pulled out a business card to give him.

"I have no card," he said.

"What do you do for a living?"

"Well, for the last few years, I've done virtually nothing. I assure you that I did everything I could to survive the situation in which I found myself.

"I was just released from prison. I'm on my way home to New Jersey, where my wife and children are waiting."

There was sudden silence.

"Don't worry," he added. "I'm not a bad person."

She cleared her throat and said, "I'm sorry."

"It's OK. I could have been one of your projects. I wrote you a few years ago to ask for your help in proving my innocence. You answered that your priority was cases for prisoners on death row. As my case didn't qualify, you weren't able to help. It took me a long time to prove my innocence, but here I am, free and sitting beside a beautiful woman."

"The truth is, I don't know what to say. I'm not sure if I should commiserate or congratulate you."

"Either one is fine." He smiled.

"Congratulations, then. I'm glad you made it happen. It's not an easy thing to do."

During the flight, Tony summarized his criminal trial, explaining how some corrupt prosecutors and a criminal gang called the El Dorado Task Force committed various crimes to obtain his guilt, including perjury, obstruction of justice, and witness intimidation.

He explained he established one of the leading companies in the market of remittances in the New York metropolitan area and how the government destroyed it to favor Western Union and Money Gram. He told her how police officers tampered with tape-recorded conversations and added how the same officers were finally caught and charged with their crimes.

The flight landed on time at JFK. Roanne was incredibly happy to have met Tony and asked him to keep in touch, reminding him of her number on the card.

CHAPTER NINE

The ghost of his past followed him every moment. Although he proved his innocent before the Court, society kept condemning him. Each day was more difficult than the last. Day after day, he sought work to support his family. Sometimes, it seemed he got the job only to be rejected once the firm checked his background and saw he'd been involved in a criminal trial, although that was supposed to be removed from his records.

Eight months passed after his release. He remained a prisoner of society's unconscious prejudice. He was extremely disappointed and had only the support of his wife and children. All his friends were gone long before his release.

One morning, he thought he found a solution when he recalled meeting Roanne. She could help him without worrying about any prejudice. When he called, she was glad to hear from him.

"You probably won't believe this," she told him, "but the truth is, I've been talking about you every week since we met on the plane. Despite the fact we don't take cases unless they involve the death penalty, which was why we couldn't take your case at the time, I wanted to convince my superiors to include all criminal cases regardless of what sentence the accused faced.

"For years I've heard that over 400,000 innocent prisoners are serving sentences in the U.S., while another 450,000 have sentences that are greater than those authorized by law. In addition, more than 10,000 innocent people are sent to prison every year. I did an analysis and was terrified to find one piece of information on the Internet. It turns out the 97% of defendants who are brought before a jury are found guilty. That sounds unreasonable. When two parties face each other in court, no matter in which field, the results should be closer to 50-50. It shouldn't be 97% and 3%. It's clear what's happening in our system."

"That's what we need, Roanne, people who can see reality. We shouldn't accept the testimony of prosecutors and police officers unless they are subjected to proper scrutiny. It's difficult to understand why, but they lie constantly to get convictions. They present fake witnesses, tamper with, and sometimes alter evidence.

"I know from my own experience. Drew Houlihan, one of the officers in charge of the investigation in the case the government fabricated against me, lied on at least five occasions that I can prove. What's worse, he tampered with several recordings of the case, which were key to the jury finding me guilty. I refer specifically to tape recording 104. It's clear how it was altered and how rotten the system is, as well as how corrupt the officers are. Experts can confirm what I say. Just ask that the tape recordings be tested.

"I like the idea that you might cover all such cases, but remember it's not just about freeing the innocent. It should also be about punishing the guilty. Those prosecutors, police, and fake witnesses are guilty of destroying lives and families based on falsehoods and violations of the law. Those are crimes, too, worse that the crimes committed by those who are called criminals, because they know the law. If they aren't severely punished, they'll continue to commit those crimes. This is the only country where I've seen crimes committed in order to arrest supposed criminals. In reality, they're arresting innocent people."

"Let's have dinner and continue this conversation."

"I'd like to, but to be honest, I have other priorities right now. I'm still out of work, which is why I called you. I wanted to ask if you'd accept my résumé in case a job opportunity presents itself for something you could refer me. I understand you don't know me well, but I wouldn't disappoint you."

"Perfect. That's another reason to have dinner together. By the way, I have a meeting with some people who are interested in financing our project. I'm sure once we get the funding, we'll need human resources. You might fit in there. Bring your résumé with you. The meeting's tomorrow night at nine o'clock. Call me tomorrow, and I'll give you the address."

"I'll call around six. Is that OK?"

"Perfect."

"OK. I'll call."

"'Bye, Tony."

CHAPTER TEN

Tony, opening a drawer on his small desk, took out one of the many copies of his curriculum vitae he prepared. He read it over carefully, dropped down to a brown couch in front of the desk, and felt convinced all his efforts were in vain.

He studied several college careers and participated in specialized programs in universities of prestige in the U.S. He also had business experience and was fluent in several languages, but none of it helped. He lived in a society that condemned him even after he was proven innocent. He still didn't have a decent job to support his family, although he had the spark that enabled him to keep going—his wife and family.

He yielded to tiredness and went to his bedroom to flop onto the bed beside his wife. She stroked his face and settled into his arms.

In the morning, he took the children to school and returned to the house to say good-bye to his wife, who had to go to work. The day passed without any novelty, no different from any other day, except he would meet with Roanne. For some reason, he felt he might find a job.

He called her at 6:00 as agreed, and she told him to meet her at 8:30 and gave him the address he needed. He dressed quickly, choosing a dark-blue suit with white shirt, black shoes, and a blue-and-red tie.

The restaurant was near his New Jersey home. He took Route 4 to the Hackensack exit and soon arrived at the restaurant. Although it took only fifteen minutes to get there, he spent another ten looking for parking. The restaurant was in a diverse mall with many spaces reserved for those who came to eat. He finally found a very isolated spot some distance away, where a three-foot fence separated the parking area from small woods at the back of the building.

Although she told him to meet her at 8:30, he arrived at 8:00. He sat at the bar and asked for tea with lemon, which was served even though he was at the bar. He assumed he would remain there until Roanne arrived, but, to his surprise, he turned and saw her already there, accompanied by two others. She beckoned him over to her table.

"Hi, Roanne," Tony said. "How are you?"

"I'm doing fine. May I introduce Mr. Gabriel?"

"A pleasure. My name's Tony Parker."

"The pleasure is mine."

"This is his wife, Sarah."

"Hi, Sarah. A pleasure."

"Hi. Please sit down," Sarah said.

"I've already told them about you," Roanne said, "but we haven't addressed the reason why you're here tonight. We've been talking about you and the beauty of this place."

They were in a Brazilian restaurant famous for the variety of the meat served in a single order. Customers paid twenty dollars and ate until full. They could also enjoy a tasty sangria, a fresh salad bar, and Creole rice, all included in the price.

It was a busy place, and the ample parking helped attract customers, who appreciated not having to worry about parking spaces like in New York City.

The interior was enormous. Candles on the tables and large lamps hanging from the ceiling gave plenty of light, adding a Christmas air even in the autumn with many colorful bulbs. Beautiful women approached tables every two minutes to offer the customers meat of their choice. All wore wine-colored skirts and tops, as if the costumes were designed to match the carpet.

It was a lovely atmosphere. In other circumstances, Tony would have enjoyed it to the fullest. Maybe someday he could bring his family there.

The conversation was interesting. Gabriel and Sarah were impressed with the summary Tony made of the government's criminal case against him. It seemed as if his case was the only reason they were there, but it wasn't. There was another reason the couple wanted to commit themselves to the project. Roanne didn't need her perfect lexicon to convince them. They seem to have already reached a decision and simply needed a reason to move forward. In exchange, they wanted to remain anonymous.

Eventually Gabriel and Sarah left, although

they stopped to speak with some others at the continuous table. They were greeted warmly, and Sarah mentioned the last time she saw the girl was when she still played with dolls. It turned out it was the girl's sixteenth birthday. They were apparently a wealthy family, or they had important government positions, as shown by the obvious security guards in the room. Two muscular men in black stood at either side of the table. Wires ran from under their suit coats to their ears. A nearby side table was also occupied by security guards, who spent their time scanning the others in the restaurant.

Gabriel and Sarah finally said good-bye to the family and left.

"What was your impression of them?" Roanne asked Tony.

"It seems they're already committed to the project. They acted as if their decision was made before they came here, but I must be honest with you. I think behind their decision is some form of resentment. They talked as if their financing represented a chance for revenge against someone or something.

"Do you remember Sarah asking, 'It's not only to free those guys. It's to make them pay for all the damage?' It sounded like they were interested in rescuing those people from the government's clutches and then taking justice in their own hands."

Roanne smiled. "It's not quite like that. Sarah's comment matches your idea not only to release the innocent but punish the guilty. She referred to the guilty ones, those corrupt officials who should be reported and forced to repair the damage they caused to all those innocent people in prison, as well as their families."

"If you knew the circumstances under which I met Gabriel and Sarah, you'd understand."

"Tell me."

"Wait. I'll tell you, but first, I need to visit the ladies' room. I'll be right back."

She returned a few minutes later and saw Tony being impatient. "Are you OK?"

He just had a thought. Under other circumstances, he'd never let a lady pay his bill, but that day was an exception. Plus, her organization should pay it, anyway.

“Yeah, I’m OK,” he replied.

“Let me tell you about Sarah and Gabriel. My boss assigned me a case where the boy was sentenced to death, and the execution day was near. He was accused of setting fire to his house to kill his three children, who were between three and six years old. The Government convinced the jury that his motive was jealousy for his wife, who wanted to abandon them. The Government also presented scientists as witnesses who claimed the fire was deliberate.

“Due to the short time before the execution, we rushed to reexamine the physical evidence of the case. We went over it repeatedly and hired seven different experts. All agreed that the fire was accidental. I remember the excitement generated by each result from our working group.

“Convinced by those reports and that our client was unjustly accused, we tried to stop the execution until we could get a court date and prove his innocence. To everyone’s surprise, the governor denied our request to delay.

“That was frustrating, and I had to tell our

client. Can you imagine having to tell someone that we had two different pieces of news—we proved he was innocent, but he would be executed anyway?

"While I sat in the visiting room, awaiting his arrival, I was sweating. My hands shook like the room was below zero. I felt impotent and thought instead of being in there, I should be knocking on doors until someone listened to me. When I left the office, our team was making calls to members of Congress and the media to see if anyone could stop the execution, but no one was interested. I felt as if my head would explode.

"Then two people approached me and told me to stay calm. They knew the two pieces of information and had already told the prisoner. It was Gabriel and Sarah, his parents. I had spoken with them on the phone, but I never met them.

"I felt a huge sense of relief mixed with guilt. When the prisoner walked in, it was amazing to see him so calm when the rest of us were upset. It seemed he was resigned to his fate. I remember what he said very clearly.

"'I can't deny that I still hope for a miracle. However, if it doesn't happen, for some reason, I still feel at peace. There's a spiritual peace I've never felt before. That's what I asked God for, and apparently, He gave it to me.'

"I told him we were still making calls and knocking on doors, and I, too, was hoping for a miracle. He told me that it didn't matter what happened. He was grateful.

"Then he added, 'I want you to know that I thank you and your organization for the promptness with which you acted. I should have asked you for help before and not listened to my lawyer. Obviously, your research results haven't pleased certain people, and I think the result would have been the same. They prefer to live with their dirty conscience rather than admit they were wrong.'

"They executed him, Tony. They killed him!"

"On what grounds did the governor base his decision to deny an application for a stay of execution?"

"You won't believe this. He argued that the

state had spent a lot of money on the case already, and the evidence was overwhelming. It didn't matter that the best-accredited person in the world had written him a letter ensuring that the fire was accidental."

"The media didn't try to stop it?"

"Every media company denied us the opportunity to spread the word about an innocent man being executed. However, the execution itself was broadcast everywhere. They gave it huge coverage. CNN dedicated hours of programming to it. I understand that their purpose is to make money, not ensure justice. Does that help you understand Gabriel and Sarah?"

"Not only do I understand them, but I also feel sorry for them."

"Today God gave them the opportunity to be in a position where they can help. It seems as if their son, Gabi, is helping from heaven. It's amazing that when he was originally charged, they didn't have the money to hire a good lawyer. They had to fight the government with a public attorney.

Chapter VI

"I remember speaking to that man. He was arrogant and indifferent to the pain of others. He was totally evil. He knew Gabi was innocent, but to maintain his professional reputation as good counsel, he preferred to remain silent when he found out after the trial that Gabi was innocent. He didn't want to keep fighting to stop the execution. On the contrary, he explicitly stated that Gabi was guilty. Today, Sarah and Gabriel are wealthy. His communications business is very prosperous.

"They want to help free the innocent and ensure that the guilty ones are charged. For that, they're trying to change state and federal laws in Congress. The gentleman who was at the side table when they left, the man they spoke with, is committed to their cause. He's Senator Dole from New York State. I'm not sure about the details, but his bill has the main objective of removing the immunity of police and prosecutors in cases where there are clear violations of the law."

She paused. "Let's talk about you now. I think conditions are right for you to come work with us. When I get into the office on Monday, I'll speak with my superiors. Did you bring your CV?"

"Yes. Here." He handed it to her.

Roanne paid the bill, and they left the restaurant. Tony walked her to her car. She said good-bye and kissed his cheek, stroking his arm as a sign of support.

Tony walked to where his car was parked and met three young men. Two sat on the trunk of a black Trans-Am sitting ten cars from his own Nissan Maxima. A third young man sat on the pavement. All three had beer cans in their hands, and they looked suspicious.

One of them, with difficulty, asked in Spanish, "*Como ta, amigo?*"

"Very well," Tony replied.

All three were Caucasian who seemed very carefree. Their long hair and disorderly beards made them seem older, but they were only nineteen or twenty. They kept looking at each other and around, checking out their surroundings. Tony was certain they were planning something.

He was ready to open his car door when the

silence of the night was shattered by a car alarm. A black Mercedes and a black Jeep prepared to leave the parking lot. The young men were sitting in that area.

Suddenly, police cars arrived, their lights flashing. One approached the source of the alarm and saw the three young men removing the last tire from the Trans-Am.

The three men ran off. One of them fired a gun at the police. In seconds, confusion took over, and police responded with gunfire.

The young men ran toward Tony, and the police kept firing as if they wanted to unload their guns completely. In the middle of the mêlée, the black Mercedes Benz sped out of its parking place only to be blocked by the police cars.

The occupants of the black Jeep got out and ran to the Mercedes, opening the doors and yanking out the occupants. The hysterical woman cried desperately, as the boys moved her from the scene and hid behind a car. One walked off with a cell phone in his hands.

Tony watched the scene evolve from his position. When he saw the young men coming his way, he jumped the fence and disappeared into the woods. The young men followed in the same direction.

Tony, hiding behind a tree, saw one of the boys draw his gun while running, with the others right behind. Police officers jumped the fence and chased them. A few seconds later, the area was flooded with police cars, and a helicopter flew overhead, its spotlights illuminating the night, leading the officers on the ground to the boys.

Tony stepped out of hiding, intending to report the direction the thieves took when he met the police. Instead of listening to him, they aimed their guns at him, and the helicopter took position overhead.

"Raise your hands! On your knees!"

Tony obeyed. Once he was on his knees something struck his back, then he felt a blow to his stomach and head. At least six officers beat him, while another one handcuffed him. He tried to speak but couldn't manage.

As he lost consciousness, he heard someone say into a radio, "We got him."

Chapter VI

He woke in a hospital and found he was handcuffed at the hands and feet to the bed. A thick chain around his waist made sure he was immobilized.

Two detectives were in the room, wearing side arms, whispering together. Tony was in pain, but he remembered everything perfectly.

"What day is it?" he asked.

No one spoke.

A nurse came in to check him.

"What day is it?" he asked her.

"It's Saturday." She cleaned his facial wounds, which he hadn't noticed until that time.

"I need to go to the bathroom."

She motioned to the detectives, who accompanied him. He remained handcuffed. Tears came to his eyes when he saw his reflection in the mirror. He bit his lip, trying to contain his sobs and thought of his wife and children.

After he used the bathroom, he was taken back to the bed, where he asked to make a phone call. She looked at the detectives, who shook their heads.

Taking advantage of the nurse's presence

as a witness, he asked the men, "If I'm handcuffed, is it because I'm under arrest, correct?"

"Yes," one said.

"Then I want to talk to a lawyer." He knew once he was under arrest, he had the right to make a phone call. He didn't think they would allow him to do it, but he needed the nurse's presence to confirm his question and their reply.

"We aren't authorized to allow you to make a call," one said.

"I can do it," the nurse said.

They shook their heads.

Tony looked her in the eyes, his expression showing everything. Then he spoke in Spanish to ask if she had aspirin. He repeated the question several times, knowing she didn't speak Spanish.

She looked for a pencil and paper, so he could write his request. He wrote *aspirin,* then added his wife's phone number. She smiled and nodded.

Barely an hour later, he was transferred to a local court. They entered the building from the rear and parked underground. The officers got him out of the vehicle and prepared to enter the building when a car stopped in front of them.

A man got out and identified himself as FBI. Tony stood calmly at the door while the policemen walked a few steps away to speak to the FBI agents. They were busy calling on the radio. Finally, they surrendered Tony to the FBI.

Despite not being told anything, Tony knew the FBI had just taken over his case. It was obvious all of them believed he was the antagonist in the incident in the parking lot.

They went into the building to an office. Tony, remaining handcuffed, stood outside while the FBI agents spoke to a person sitting at a desk. Their gestures indicated a heated discussion. At one moment, the officer at the desk jumped and slapped his computer screen, saying clearly, "I will not book him."

The desk officer refused to book Tony in his present physical condition, because his face was still bleeding. Finally, he agreed only on the condition that Tony be photographed and the agents sign a document the officer wrote.

Tony was transferred to a cell. A few minutes later, his handcuffs were removed. He was forced to change out of his bloody clothes and wear an orange outfit with blue sneakers.

Photos were taken of his injuries, and each agent signed on the back. They also took his fingerprints, then more photos to create a prisoner file. An hour later, he was transferred to what they called a Special Housing Unit, a solitary cell where prisoners could be mentally tortured.

Tony remained there until Monday morning when he was transferred to an office where a man in a suit and tie waited for him—his lawyer. Without asking for one, he had been assigned a government lawyer.

He introduced himself and produced a business card. "I'll be representing you during this process. There will be a preliminary hearing where you'll be informed of the charges the government alleges against you."

With each passing moment, it became increasingly clear that Tony was being accused of the entire incident on Friday night. The lawyer didn't ask any questions. When Tony tried to describe the events of Friday night, the lawyer wasn't interested. Their conversation was limited to the lawyer telling Tony there would be time for Tony to give him the details later.

When they entered a courtroom, many memories flooded into Tony's mind. He never thought he'd face a courtroom full of people again.

When he heard a child say, "Daddy," his eyes flooded with tears, and he bit his lip. He stared at his children and wife, shaking his head in confusion. Hoping the situation would be cleared up soon, he motioned for his wife not to worry.

"All rise," the clerk said.

The judge came in from the robing room.

"The Honorable Judge Kenneth Kaplan is presiding."

"What do we have today?" the judge asked.

"Case number 00-Cr-2464, *United States v. Tony Parker.*"

"Is the Government ready to proceed?"

The prosecutor stood and said, "Yes, Your Honor." He was a man in his late twenties named

Cain Caiaphas. He stood five-feet-eight-inches tall, wearing a gray suit and red tie. His white shirt shone as if ironed with starch. His black shoes shone from a recent polish. Blond hair and blue eyes made it obvious he was Caucasian.

"Your Honor, the Government of the United States accused Mr. Parker of attempted theft of private property, aggression to an authority in the exercise of its duties, and the murder of young Ashley Dole."

Tony's legs began shaking. He never knew anyone died in the incident. He gave his lawyer a confused look, but the man ignored him. Tony's bewilderment wasn't due to the crimes he'd been charged with. It was the realization that even with the severity of the incident, the Government wasn't interested in opening a thorough investigation of the events. He calmed himself by thinking that he had nothing to do with the incident and expected he wouldn't have to wait eleven years as he did earlier to prove his innocence.

The judge continued reading the charges line by line from a document supported by the affidavits of the officers who participated in the arrest. A murmur went up in the courtroom. Tony looked back, fearing for the safety of his wife and children, then calmed himself when he saw several agents in the room.

At the end of the reading of the charges, the judge looked at Tony. “How does the accused plead?”

“Not guilty, Your Honor,” Tony said.

David Ppaz, Tony’s lawyer, who hadn’t said a word so far, finally addressed the court. “Your Honor, the defense requests that my client be released on bail. He is a person with extraordinarily strong roots in this country. His wife and children were U.S. citizens who reside in New Jersey. He is a national of this country. A bail of $100,000 can guarantee this request. He isn’t someone who is a flight risk.”

“Request denied. You forgot to mention that your client represents a danger to society.”

The judge didn’t wait for the prosecutor to oppose the request, showing the level of prejudice in the case.

“The next hearing will be held on November

16 at three o'clock. By then, each party must submit any requests to the court. This court is adjourned."

The judge walked out, as did the prosecutor and Tony's attorney, who left without saying good-bye. That didn't upset him. He knew of the contempt anyone who was accused of a crime by the U.S. government was subject to, even with the falsehood that someone was innocent until proven guilty. The first person to demonstrate that contempt was usually the defendant's counsel. Tony knew a lawyer's oath was nothing more than a way to cover prejudice.

Most lawyers don't take up the profession to seek justice, he thought. *They choose justice to make money.*

He said good-bye to his wife and children with a look. Once again, he told them in gestures not to worry. He saw everything very simply, although he didn't think he would go through the same injustice of the American system twice.

November 16 arrived. Only then, despite calls he and his family placed to him, was he able to speak to him. Mr. Ppaz arrived at his cell at 2:45 PM. Tony was awakened at 3:00 AM to be taken to the courtroom, and he was tired. All he'd eaten was a piece of bread with less than an ounce of bologna an officer gave him. He was hungry and thirsty and wore handcuffs when his lawyer arrived. Thick glass separated them, but they heard each other's voices clearly.

"As you know, today is the hearing," Ppaz said.

"I've tried unsuccessfully to communicate with you all this time. My wife has also tried without success. I think fifteen minutes isn't enough time to prepare."

"Our defense is extremely limited. The government has overwhelming evidence against you. In addition, there are several witnesses. That doesn't even count the testimony of the officers who were at the scene of the crime.

"My advice to you is that I've reviewed all your documents. You weren't read your rights, which I believe is reason enough to dismiss the case. It's the only legal basis we have. Today I'll bring a motion asking that your case be dismissed based on that flaw. If we don't succeed with that, I recommend you plead guilty as soon as possible to avoid the death penalty. I'm sure the prosecutor would agree in order to avoid a long, costly trial."

"Mr. Ppaz, you haven't even heard my version of events, and you're already recommending I plead guilty? That seems professionally dishonest. Concerning the motion you're about to submit, I forbid you to give such a document to the court."

"That's your only legal argument. Are you asking me not to raise it?"

"Yes. I don't want you to raise this issue for two reasons. First, I know the only reason you prepared the motion is to justify the check you'll receive from the government for this case. I also know the motion won't be approved.

"Second, I don't want to leave prison based on legal technicalities. I'm innocent of the charges. Only after proving my innocence do I want to get out of here. You don't seem interested in knowing I'm innocent."

"It's your decision. I'll see you in court." He

stood and walked out.

At three o'clock that afternoon, the courtroom was empty when Tony was brought in. It felt like only seconds when he looked again to see the place was packed. His wife and children sat in first row. Roanne was there, too. Tony was surprised to see Gabriel and Sarah with her.

Silence filled the room when the judge's door opened.

"All rise!" the clerk said.

"Judge Kaplan presiding over this case, *U.S. v. Tony Parker,* docket number 2464."

"Good afternoon," the judge said. "What do we have today?"

"Your Honor," Ppaz said, "the defense asks the court to withdraw the charges, because the rights of Mr. Parker were not read at the time of his arrest. Mr. Parker...."

Tony jumped up from his seat. "Your Honor, with all due respect, I ask to be heard." He continued without being given permission. "I gave specific instructions to this lawyer that his motion was not to be submitted. He just did so without my consent. This generates a conflict of interest, and on that basis, I ask that this lawyer be removed from this case."

"For the record," the judge said, "you might wish to specify the reasons why you don't want the motion submitted."

"Yes, Your Honor. My reasons are simple. I don't want to get out of prison based on legal technicalities, although I'm sure Your Honor would not approve such a motion. Forget the law and my rights. I want to discuss the facts of what really happened the night of the incident."

The prosecutor looked at Tony as if his heart said something different from his thoughts.

"I ask that you allow me to represent myself before this court."

"Are you sure of that decision?"

"Yes, Your Honor."

"Do you waive your constitutional right to be represented by a lawyer?"

"I waive my right to be represented by an ineffective lawyer, not my right to be represented by an effective one, which is what the court should provide me."

Chapter VI

The prosecutor finally intervened. He knew that was sufficient reason to appeal the case, since the law was very clear in that regard. Tony should be represented by an effective lawyer, and it was obvious even to the prosecutor that Mr. Ppaz was not effective.

"Your Honor," the prosecutor said, "the best course of action must be to appoint another lawyer to Mr. Parker."

"I agree," the judge said. "Wait to be contacted by your new lawyer, Mr. Parker. This session ends."

A new lawyer didn't arrive. However, Roanne accompanied by five boys visited Tony in prison. All were twenty-five or younger, and all dressed informally in sport shoes, jeans, and short-sleeved Polo shirts. One wore a New York Mets cap.

Roanne also dressed informally, wearing tennis shoes, tight jeans that showed her well-formed butt, and a white blouse that was nearly transparent. Her nipples showed clearly through her bra. She was beautiful and had an angelic face.

"Hello, Tony." She kissed his cheek and hugged him. "This is Eric, Carlos, Bernie, Robert, and, finally, Roy. Boys, this is Tony."

"A pleasure," Tony said.

"Your case has been taken up by our organization," she said. "We've been assigned to this project, but only if you want us."

"I was willing to represent myself to avoid being sunk by an irresponsible lawyer, but that doesn't mean I don't realize I need help. What do you have in mind?"

"The first thing is, we believe you're innocent," Bernie said.

"That's right," the other four chorused.

Roanne looked at him. "That's a good start."

CHAPTER ELEVEN

Sitting in the white mansion, as Louis read the report of Tony's life, the agent leaned into the couch and said, "I don't know why, but something tells me this man is innocent."

"Why do you say that?" Louis asked.

"Give me one reason why this young woman Roanne and those boys not only took the case but treated him like a friend even after hearing the charges. In addition, I know your people. They were blinded by malice."

"It wouldn't surprise me to know they accused him knowing he was innocent. They do that all the time. More than ten thousand innocent people go to prison each year, and my people celebrate that. Let's continue the report."

"Let's start work," Roanne said.

"What's next?" Tony asked.

"Let' not define our defense. It seems premature for that. We still have more hearings."

CHAPTER TWELVE

The government prepared to define how to proceed in the case. The prosecutor was in the lab, waiting for results of the analysis that would determine if Tony's fingerprints were on the weapon recovered from the small wood where Tony was arrested, the weapon allegedly used to kill Dole.

The technician walked up with a blue folder and handed it to the prosecutor. He was disappointed to find the results. The fingerprints weren't Tony's.

He took the folder and left the lab, returning to his office and placed on his desktop all the evidence that was collected so far. He had police affidavits, testimony from Ashley's father, the firearm, and the cartridges from the bullets that were fired, including the one that killed young Dole. He was puzzled why Tony's clothes were included. Why hadn't they been sent to his family?

The prosecutor wondered how a truck rim thief wore a suit and tie. To bring Tony to trial required a motive, and that motive was the theft of tires. He looked at the evidence again. The case was weak, and he concluded that he needed to open another investigation so more evidence could be collected.

The following day, the prosecutor went to his boss' office and presented his concerns, requesting a thorough investigation of the case. Not only did he feel the evidence was weak, but he suspected Tony wasn't guilty.

"Mr. Julianni, having said all that," the prosecutor finished, "I think another investigation is the best course of action."

The DA's anger was so great, it seemed that all his blood accumulated in his head, making it turn red. His hands trembled with rage.

"I've made it clear to you since the beginning that this case must end quickly with someone in jail," the DA said.

"That's what I mean, Sir. I agree that it should end quickly, but as you say, the guilty person must be sent to jail. I'm not sure of the guilt of the man who's in prison."

"Explain yourself."

"Mr. Parker's fingerprints aren't on the gun. Although it might seem trivial, I find it hard to believe that a truck rim thief would wear a suit and tie. This morning I was given a separate report that told me the ballistics analysis on Mr. Parker came back negative."

The DA gestured to indicate he understood his assistant's comments, although he hid his reactions carefully. "We have sufficient evidence. Take it to trial and end this once and for all. I've already received 99 letters from that place and 435 from another. You know what I mean. We have too much pressure. Those fucking criminals don't know how to choose their victims."

The assistant DA left the office feeling bewildered. He was just told to finish the case no matter who was sent to jail, even if it was an innocent man.

News headlines echoed the DA's thoughts.

Justice in Death of

Daughter of Robert Dole

Senator Dole calls for

Justice

To Act Fast

Chapter VI

They Will Take to Trail
the
Killer of Dole's Daughter

He Acted in Retaliation
Against
The System for Keeping
Him in
Prison Unjustly

However, *Le Monde* in France gave information on the evidence that leaked from the prosecutor's office.

Dole Case, USA: Fingerprints Do Not
Match, Ballistics Test Negative

Publication of that article caught national attention in the U.S. What had seemed a strong case for the prosecution quickly became unclear, and opinions from legal analysts were divided.

Nancy Grace, famous for finding all defendants guilty before trial, gave the following answer when asked if Tony was guilty: "What I know today is that the daughter of Mr. Dole is dead. Who killed her? I don't know."

The prosecutor returned to the lab and met technicians who were assigned to Tony's case. He asked the analysis to be repeated.

"That's not necessary," the leader of the group said. "That report was consistent with the first two. It was actually the third test we ran."

"Congressional pressure is strong," the prosecutor said. "Is there any possibility the fingerprints were erased?"

"Let's assume that happened," one of the team said. "What happened to the ballistics test? Was that also deleted?"

The prosecutor looked at the person. "Is that a possibility?"

"Yes."

"Then make it appear in the report." He left the room.

The trial began after jury selection was finished. The final jury was completely made up of Caucasians. A young Hispanic woman who was selected was later disqualified for being only nineteen years old. The prosecutor argued she was too young for such a responsibility, ignoring the law that stated the only requirement was to be over the age of eighteen.

The courtroom was packed. Tony's wife and children were there. Roanne was present with Eric, Roy, Robert, Carlos, and Bernie. Another man accompanied her wearing a black hat and a cane. He was at least eighty-years old, but he looked strong and serene despite the cane. He sat beside Tony, while Roanne and the boys sat on the other side. When she greeted Tony, she held his left hand against the table.

"We need experience to defend you in this courtroom," she said. "That's why Mr. Randolph accompanied us. Don't worry. You're in good hands."

The first day of the trail passed without the government submitting anything new or different from information already in the public domain. This included introducing the members of the jury, who had previously been admitted before the judge during *voir dire* before being selected. The prosecution explained how all the details of the case were followed. Opening statements from both sides was more of the same things that everyone already knew.

Officer Rivera was the last to testify that day. His testimony was substantially the same as the police officers who testified before him. He and his partner were the first to arrive at the scene of the crime on that Friday night.

"Mr. Rivera, for whom do you work?" the prosecutor asked.

"I'm an officer of the State of New Jersey Police Department."

"Mr. Rivera, where were you the night of the incident where young Dole lost her life? Were you on duty that evening?"

"Yes, I was on duty that night. I was with my partner in a liquor store on Teaneck Avenue, playing the Mega Lotto."

"Did you receive an emergency call requesting your presence at a shopping mall in Hackensack, New Jersey?"

"That is correct."

Chapter VI

"Did you show up at that place?"

"Yes. My partner and I arrived on the scene as quickly as we could."

"Officer Rivera, could you explain to the jury how events transpired? Please sit a little closer to the microphone. Thank you."

Officer Rivera cleared his throat and began speaking. "In the beginning, everything seemed in order when we arrived. A few cars were coming in and out of the large parking area. We began searching from one side to the other. The 911 call didn't specify exactly where the robbery was taking place. It was just reported as a robbery at the mall.

"When we came to the far end of the parking lot, I saw a parked car had flashing lights, which meant the car's alarm system was activated. As we moved closer, another patrol car arrived. Once there, I saw the car had been stripped of its tires. That was when I heard shots. My immediate reaction was to remove my gun and start shooting. My partner did the same."

"At whom were you shooting?"

The officer hesitated, as if looking for the

right response. Finally, he said, "I shot at someone running from the area where I heard the shots come from."

"Had you identified that person?"

"Not at that moment. It was a little dark, and I was at a distance."

"You said a moment ago that you shot the person who ran from that place. Why couldn't you identify him?"

"He was moving away from us. I only saw his back, not his face."

"Continue your narration."

"Once we started shooting, I heard others shooting toward where the person was going. Then I got up and started to advance, along with the other police officers, who were already there, in the direction the people ran. We jumped a small fence that separated the parking lot from some small woods. A helicopter illuminated the area ahead of us. In the woods, suddenly a subject appeared before us. He came out from behind a tree. He said something, but I don't remember what.

"When we approached him, we identified

ourselves as police officers and handcuffed him. When he resisted arrest, we used special tactics to subdue him. Once he was neutralized, we transported him to a hospital, where he remained until Monday. Upon leaving the hospital, we took him into custody. However, FBI agents met us to arrest him. It was only until that moment that I participated in his capture."

"Agent Rivera, the person you saw running and then resisting arrest, who was then taken to the hospital, and a few days later was transferred into your detention, was then arrested by the FBI—is that person in this courtroom?"

"Yes, Sir."

"Can you identify him?"

"Yes. He's the gentleman in the orange uniform beside the young lady dressed in gray, sitting behind your table."

"Thank you."

It was the defense's turn to cross-examine the witness. Agent Rivera seemed calm, but he was obviously concerned. He blinked rapidly and rubbed his hands as if nervous.

Mr. Randolph was ready to begin his

questions when the prosecutor noticed the policeman's nervousness and called for a recess, which was granted.

During the ten-minute recess, the prosecutor approached Rivera to make sure he was all right. "Are you OK? I saw you looking a bit concerned."

"No, Sir. I'm just a bit exhausted. Everything is OK."

When court began again, Mr. Randolph approached the policeman. "Agent Rivera, I don't have to introduce myself. We already know each other, right?"

"Yes."

"Agent, you were the first to arrive at the scene, correct?"

"Yes."

"When you came to the spot where the car had its lights flashing, did you approach the car?"

"Before reaching it, I heard gunshots. I stopped to respond to them."

"You testified it was dark, and the distance prevented you from identifying the person who was running and shooting, correct?"

"Yes, Sir."

"A few minutes ago, the prosecutor asked you to identify that person, and you indicated it was Mr. Tony Parker. Correct?"

"Yes, Sir."

"Once in the woods, at the time you used special techniques to subdue him, how did you know he was the subject who'd been shooting?"

"It was obvious. He was the only person there."

"My question is whether you're sure Mr. Parker was the person who'd been shooting?"

"He was the only one there."

"Once you heard the shots, you said in your testimony that you got up. What do you mean by that? Where did you get up from?"

The policeman hesitated, then said, "I positioned myself on the ground to shoot at the subjects."

"Subjects? I thought it was a single subject, who you identified as Mr. Parker."

"Did I say subjects? I was wrong. I meant to say the subject."

"You also said in your testimony the

following. Let me quote it exactly. 'Then I got up and started to advance along with the other police officers who were already there, in the direction where they ran.' Were you wrong again, Officer?"

The agent's nervousness increased. "I meant to say where he had run."

"You made a mistake?"

"That's correct."

"You testified that you don't remember what Mr. Parker said when he came out of hiding. However, you remember everything else perfectly, from the time when you were in the liquor store playing Mega Lotto until the FBI agents came. Why don't you remember what he said?"

"I don't remember."

"Officer, you testified for the prosecution in the case of *The People v. Agustin-Garcia,* saying that when you arrived at the scene of the crime, you listened to how Mr. Garcia was discharging his weapon into the body of Mrs. Ricart. However, a recording taken during the incident showed you arrived at the scene ten minutes after that happened. Can you explain that, Officer Rivera?"

"Objection!" the prosecutor said.

"Overruled," the judge said.

"Can you answer my question?" Mr. Randolph said.

"Answer the question," the judge said.

"I arrived and saw how some people were struggling with Mr. Garcia and thought I heard shooting at that time."

"Obviously, you were wrong, correct?"

"Yes."

"Could it have happened the same way in this case, Officer Rivera? Did you see and hear things incorrectly?"

"I don't think so."

"Your Honor, the defense offers the defendant's Exhibit A, showing a completely different version to what Agent Rivera has said."

The prosecutor was very disconcerted. The exhibit was a video recording of the full incident at the mall parking lot. It clearly showed that Rivera and his partner, once they heard the first shot, hid behind a car. All their shots were fired into the air. They never once saw their target.

The recording also showed how three young men ran in the same direction Tony went. It was true that it couldn't be distinguished who fired the weapon, although it was noticeably clear Tony hadn't done it. The camera captured every move.

The truth was, agent Rivera could never have identified any of the subjects. He had lied in court. Four people ran off, not one, as he tried to make the jury believe.

The prosecutor, furious at being surprised by the recording, immediately submitted a motion that the judge approved. The evidence would be suppressed, because the video hadn't been submitted to the prosecution before the trial. The judge ruled it was a violation of judicial proceedings, which Mr. Randolph expected. However, he knew the jury would remember it.

The government called its last witness, although even the lab technician didn't cause much damage to the defense with his false testimony. The technician, knowing that Mr. Parker's fingerprints were not present and knowing that while in police custody Tony received a paraffin test to determine if he recently fired a gun, explained that it was possible in certain cases that those tests could come up negative even when someone fired a gun.

The next witness was devastating.

"Mr. Dole, can you identify yourself?" the prosecutor asked.

"Robert Dole."

He was a shareholder in the Federal Reserve, a bank disguised as a public institution that actually belonged to a group of bourgeois from different parts of the world. He was the father of the young woman who was killed during the events of that Friday night. One year earlier, he was elected Senator for the State of New York.

"I'm sorry for your loss," the prosecutor said. "My condolences to you and your family."

"Thank you."

"Could you describe the incident where your daughter lost her life, Sir?"

"We just finished dinner at The Grayfield, a restaurant in a shopping mall in Hackensack. We were about to leave the parking lot when we heard shooting. My family and I were in the same vehicle, accompanied by my driver, while my bodyguard followed at a short distance. Once we heard the shots, the driver rushed to leave the place, but police cars blocked the exit.

"My bodyguard came and took us out of the car. My daughter remained a few seconds longer in her seat. We realized she wasn't moving, because she was injured. Even though the ambulance picked her up within a few minutes, she later died at the hospital. The bullet pierced her heart."

"Did you see who shot your daughter?"

"No, Sir. However, a few minutes before the incident, I saw the defendant walk past us while we were about to get into our car in the parking lot. At first, he seemed like a decent person. I never thought he was a simple car thief and a killer."

"Objection, Your Honor," Randolph said.

"Sustained."

"Can you identify the defendant as the person you saw passing by you in the parking lot?"

"Yes. It's the accused, sitting over there." He pointed.

"Once again, I'm sorry for your daughter's death. By the way, how old was she when she died?"

"The next day...." He began crying. "...she would have been sixteen."

The defense began its cross-examination.

"Mr. Dole," Randolph said, "first I'd like to say I'm deeply sorry about your daughter. My name is Billy Randolph, and I represent Mr. Tony Parker. Mr. Dole, you testified that my client seemed to be a decent person. What made you think that?"

"It's not common to see a car thief wearing a suit and tie. That's what he wore when I saw him."

The prosecutor lowered his head and sighed, because he'd been thinking the same thing.

"In your honest opinion," Randolph continued, "is the fact that you saw Mr. Parker going in the same direction where the incident occurred proof that he's the car thief who murdered your daughter?"

"No, Sir."

"Mr. Dole, the evidence shows that your daughter died from a gunshot to the heart. Where was she seated at the time of the impact of the bullet?"

"She sat in the middle, between her mother and me, in the back seat of our car."

"When you were about to leave the parking lot, what direction did you take? Were you going in the same direction where the shots came from, or in the opposite direction?"

"It's difficult for me to answer. I only know I heard shooting. Where the shots came from, I don't know."

"Let me change the question. Were you going in the same direction that my client ran or in the opposite direction?"

"In the opposite direction."

"But the bullet struck your daughter's heart?"

Dole thought about that for a moment, then said, "Yes, Sir."

The situation felt strange to Dole. The police's version of events pointed to the bullet striking the rear of the vehicle, going through the back seat, striking the girl in the back, then the bullet exiting her chest and leaving a hole in the windshield.

Dole retired from the witness stand thinking something wasn't right. Mr. Randolph tried, perhaps unsuccessfully, to leave the same idea in the minds of the jury.

Up until that point, the prosecution felt sure of a victory. The biggest damage caused by the defense was the recording that demonstrated that Agent Rivera lied, but that wasn't admissible as evidence, and the judge instructed the jury not to take the recording into consideration.

CHAPTER THIRTEEN

Adolf listened carefully to the report about Tony's life. Louis paused, looking at his friend.

"What do you think about the report so far?" Louis asked.

"The truth is that you act like what you are—devilish."

"Why do you say that?"

"Think about it. A bullet penetrated the back of the vehicle, crossed through the seat, penetrated the young woman's body, pierced her heart, and then went through the windshield? Only a stupid jury would believe that."

Louis smiled. "You haven't heard the saying about a grand jury and a petit jury in this country."

"What is it?"

"Prosecutors could bring before a grand jury a ham sandwich to be charged with a crime, and they'd still issue an indictment. Worse yet, the petit jury that presided over the trial would find the ham sandwich guilty.

"The citizens of this country believe every word from our representatives in the government, especially if the defendants are Black or Hispanic or any non-Caucasian race."

Adolf was astonished. "Let's move on, Louis. I'm anxious to know the end."

CHAPTER FOURTEEN

The defense called its first witness, who looked calm and willing to offer his version of the events. For a second, he looked at his wife and children. She squeezed her son's hand while her youngest daughter embraced her, who was, in turn embraced by her older sister.

"Mr. Parker," Randolph asked, "could you describe the events that occurred the night of the incident."

He didn't bother introducing Tony to the jury, because he didn't want to tell them Tony had already been in prison for eleven years. He feared that jury would act with prejudice over that knowledge.

"I was in the Grayfield Restaurant from eight o'clock, spending nearly two hours with people who can corroborate that. I said good-bye to them and was on my way home. As I walked toward my car in the parking lot, I clearly saw three young men. Two sat on a black car, while the other sat on the pavement. One said hi to me in Spanish. I replied to the greeting and continued toward my car. Once there, I heard a car alarm go off. A minute later, I heard many shots."

As Randolph requested, Tony told the facts carefully. The jury members looked at each other in confusion, because of his clear enunciation and the precise way he recounted the facts. There was no hesitation whatsoever, and they hadn't heard his full statement before.

"Did you suffer physical injury as a result of the beating from the police during your arrest?"

"Objection, Your Honor," the prosecutor said.

"Sustain."

Although Tony suffered severe injuries, with his vision impaired by 70%, four cracked ribs, and injuries to his neck, the beating wasn't something the jury had to decide. They were there to give a verdict about the young girl's murder.

"Did you suffer any injuries that would render you unable to testify here today?"

"None that my physician has told me about."

"Were you trying to steal the rims off a

black vehicle parked in the parking lot of the Hackensack Mall on the night of the incident where Miss Dole lost her life."

"No, Sir."

"Do you recognize this weapon?" He held up a gun.

"No, Sir."

"Have you ever fired this gun?"

"No, Sir."

"Did you kill the young Miss Dole?"

"It's impossible. I've never fired a gun in my life. I don't know how to fire a gun."

"No more questions, Your Honor."

The prosecutor walked up. "Mr. Parker, you described the facts from eight o'clock in the Grayfield Restaurant until you woke in the hospital, but you didn't mention who else you saw in the parking lot on their way to their vehicle—the Dole family. Did you omit that for some reason? Isn't it true that you tried to hide from them so that your plan to steal the tires wouldn't be exposed?"

The prosecutor had asked Mr. and Mrs. Dole if they saw Tony in the parking lot. They answered positively, but he didn't want to suggest to the jury that they hadn't, and that Tony hadn't seen them. He knew that Tony said hello to one of the bodyguards.

"I never tried to hide," Tony replied. "On the contrary, I said hi to some of their companions."

The prosecutor, realizing his question gave the wrong effect, tried to divert the course of his questions. "Why greet them if you didn't know them?"

"It's true that I don't know them, but while I had dinner in the restaurant, they dined at the next table. Sarah and Gabriel, with whom I sat, greeted them very affectionately. I felt respect for them as friends or acquaintances of Sarah and Gabriel."

The prosecutor was even more amazed by that response. The jury grumbled when the judge reminded them to pay attention to the question from the prosecutor.

In desperation, the prosecutor went to the fact that Tony had been in federal prison for eleven years. He knew Tony was cleared of all charges but hoped to bias the jury against him. He tried to suggest Tony left prison through a stroke of luck or a technicality, not because he was truly innocent.

He kept trying to make the jury believe the motive that ended in the death of Miss Dole was money. Tony was unemployed for eight months and lacked financial resources, which explained why he tried to steal the tires. Those actions led to the young woman's death.

It seemed the jury didn't believe a single word he said. Some even slept while he spoke. They had completely lost interest in his questions of Tony.

The trial continued for another two days. Tony's wife testified. She described how she supported her family while Tony was away. She added that currently, although it was a sacrifice, she still did.

Roanne testified, too, but her testimony didn't help much. She couldn't provide a single answer to what happened after Tony said good-bye to her in the restaurant parking lot. She was already gone by the time Tony walked to his car.

Chapter VI

The same thing happened with Gabriel and Sarah, although they tried to highlight Tony's good qualities while they were with him.

The defense hired an expert to determine if the weapon contained any trace from Tony. Unlike the prosecution's expert, he stated that it wasn't possible that fingerprints had been deleted. Instead, he testified that there were, indeed, fingerprints, but they belonged to someone else, not Tony.

That didn't bother the prosecutor. His goal was to find Tony guilty. It didn't matter whose traces were on the gun.

The trial reached its final phase. The prosecutor used all his energy to convince the jury that Tony's motive for the crime was his financial situation. That was why he attempted to steal the tires. That crime resulted in the death of Miss Dole. He did his best, but it was clear even he didn't believe it.

Then came the defense's turn. Mr. Randolph told the jury that they should carefully analyze the evidence. He concentrated on the fact that the bullet that killed Miss Dole hadn't been fired by Tony, who had never used a firearm in his life. Instead, that bullet came from one of the police officers who fired.

Feeling increasingly nervous, the prosecutor immediately said, "Objection, Your Honor."

"Sustained. The Defense will abandon this theory. There is nothing in the record to prove it."

Randolph recounted each testimony, concluding that Tony was wrongfully accused, and the government hadn't performed a thorough investigation to reach the truth. If the jury didn't exercise its responsibility, the truth would be covered up with lies, and an innocent man would go to jail for life. He asked them to do justice and declare Tony innocent of all charges.

The judge read the legal procedures to the jury, and they retired to deliberate.

For the first two days, they couldn't reach an agreement on a verdict. The judge dismissed them until the following Monday at ten o'clock in the morning. They were given specific instructions not to discuss the case with anyone, much less read or listen to anything from the media about the case, which had given a lot of coverage to the story.

CHAPTER FIFTEEN

On Sunday evening in a supermarket, the president of the jury was shopping when someone approached him.

"I love these products, Mexican tortillas," the person said. "However, as days pass, I'm thinking of giving up on them."

"I don't understand," the jury president said. "You love these products, but you want to give up on them? What happened? Did they hurt you or make you gain weight?"

"In truth, no. It's a Hispanic product, and they come here only to spoil our lives. They take our jobs, kill our people, and, what's worse, there are more of them every day. They multiply like rabbits. Someday, they'll run the government."

He took out his ID and showed it to the jury president. "We need your help in the case of Miss Dole's death."

With a gesture of concern, the jury president turned and walked away, while the man stared at him.

The following Monday, Tony was found

guilty of all charges. The message from the DA reached the jury in an effective manner.

Three months later, Tony was sentenced to life in prison for the murder of Miss Dole. An additional twenty-four-month sentence was added for attempted tire theft.

"How is it looking?" Louis asked Adolf. "That's Tony. He's been in prison for three years. During that time, he lost all appeals. He wrote to every elected official in the country, as well as foreign organizations and authorities. No one listened. Roanne is the only one still trying to prove his innocence. She believes him blindly."

"Now I understand why he wants to speak with Jesus."

"Do you want me to take care of him?"

"No. Leave that for Herod to decide."

An assistant entered Louis' office with a gray folder that he handed to Louis. Louis passed it to Adolf once the assistant left.

"Well, this is the report you wanted," Louis said. "I believe our friend will realize I'm not wasting my time here on Earth. I'll be back in a few minutes. I have to take care of a few issues."

Louis left the office while Adolf studied the report. His face showed astonishment when he finished reading.

Louis was back in twenty minutes. "Sorry I'm late, Adolf. I had some personal issues."

"That's fine. I read the report about the war in Iraq. The truth is, you've got guts to go into that country to fight a war thinking they had weapons of mass destruction. If that were true, could you imagine what would have happened. All your soldiers would have died."

"Come on, Adolf. Don't be silly. The only reason I went in was because I already knew there were no weapons of mass destruction. I sent people in beforehand to make certain of that."

"And that speech given by your assistant here in the General Assembly? What's his name? Linco?"

"Ah! He's one of the clowns I use all the time. More than anyone, he knew there were no weapons of mass destruction."

"Then why'd he gave that speech?"

"He's servile."

"What was the purpose of that war?"

"My goal is clear. I want to terminate not only Jesus but all His descendants, so I can seize the Kingdom."

"Explain this attack on your military establishment. You aren't clear in the report. Was there a plane crash or not?"

"The truth is, it didn't crash. What happened was that an officer rebelled against me. He never agreed with my plan to kill so many in those buildings to justify the attack on Jesus' descendants. He wanted to react to and prevent future attacks, so he attacked my military establishment. We neutralized that in time."

"How have you convinced the world it was a terrorist attack?"

"It was easy. Sometimes, there's a lack of evidence to support real events. However, there are lies that are supported by real facts."

"What's the truth in this case? Why is there a lack of evidence?"

"The truth is that one of us wanted to destroy the Pentagon and attempted a *coup d'état.*

That's what led to the attack. This lacks evidence because we destroyed them all."

"What's the lie?"

"The lie is that it was terrorists who attacked us. However, that's supported by the destruction caused in the Pentagon and the impact of the planes against the towers."

"Tell 'em what really happened to that woman...what's her name? Ingrid Betancourt, the Colombian woman you bailed out from those Colombian guerrillas."

"That was stupidity on the part of one of my friends and the French President. They rescued her, but I never agreed with that shit for two reasons. First, they plagiarized the kidnapping. When something went wrong with the guerrilla group, it turned into something real. Those terrorists learned she was using them for political propaganda, and she'd never help legitimize them as a political group. I never agreed with that.

"The other reason is that releasing her meant kneeling at Julio Chavez' stupidity. You know my problems with him. In the end, they convinced me, and I demanded an exchange—the release of a few of my boys who'd been kidnapped."

"What happened with that girl from the CIA?"

"Oh! Her husband was responsible for that. You know how I am. Whoever isn't with me is my enemy. He refused to falsify a report about the existence of weapons of mass destruction in Iraq. I promised to get revenge against him, knowing I could hurt him. I wanted her in prison for spying in the U.S., but she's one of the best-trained and was able to determine something was being planned against her when she was sent on a ridiculous mission that was usually reserved for apprentices. When I thought she was taken prisoner, she appeared here and complained that we betrayed her."

"What did that cost you?"

"Nothing. Only one of us went to prison, and I immediately pardoned him. He didn't even serve one day in prison."

"And the presidential election in Ohio? What was that you did against your opponent? That was your second term as president, right?"

"Yes. It was my second term, which I'm still serving. We knew we'd lose the election. That state was the deciding factor in the voting. I responded in time, called in a few Russian friends, and they gave me an incredibly young boy to develop a computer program that whenever someone voted for my opponent, the program gave me the vote. No one realized the fraud, and he did all the work from Russia, too."

"What if he talks someday?"

"Adolf, don't you know me? He hasn't been able to speak for a long time. He was a good boy, but I couldn't afford any risk to my plans."

"What about the stock market? It must be really important if you're willing to allow such fraud."

"I have to admit that I'm not sure about that one. I want to leave my allies with as much money as possible to begin our new era on Earth, but I don't know if giving them that much power is wise. I want them to have possession of all those poor people's investments before I destroy them all."

"How do you get so much information about

other countries so easily? I see you're aware of everything they do."

"That's easy. I manipulated the situation so that they accept my students. Exchange programs are valid in over 200 countries. I took advantage of that and sent my informants to all those countries, posing as students."

"I understand. Why have you caused so many wars?"

"Actually, I didn't do that. My allies, in order to make fortunes, forced me to provoke those wars. They produce the weapons we use."

"What's the purpose of torturing so many people in Iraq and at that military base in Cuba?"

"That's just a method my soldiers use to release stress from the war. They're just having fun."

CHAPTER SIXTEEN

Nervousness was evident within the Heavenly Palace. Guards patrolled constantly, paying close attention to all of Jesus' and his collaborators' movements. It was seven o'clock when Adolf arrived with the summary of Tony's life and the report of Louis' activities.

In the basement, tension was high. The prisoners hadn't slept the previous night and murmured constantly to each other, watching Magdalene when she entered. She left, nervously tapping her thumb with her pencil.

All the prisoners were on alert, seizing the bars of their cell doors.

"Tell Peter we're back," Adolf told the officer who accompanied him.

"Yes, Sir."

When Adolf entered the room, he asked, "How are you, my friend?"

"Very concerned," Peter said. "Did you find out who placed the call? How much can he tell Jesus?"

"Yes, we got it, thanks to Louis' cooperation.

He said hi, by the way. Yes, the caller has a lot to tell Jesus. He's been a victim of Louis' injustice, and, because of that, I assume he knows a lot about the atrocities on Earth."

"Thank you. Do you have Louis' report?"

"Of course. Here it is. Why are you so worried?"

"I never trusted that bitch. Security surprised her trying to enter Jesus' office without being accompanied by one of our men. Luckily, they stopped her."

"I always had doubts about that woman. Even if she says no, I think she's still in love with Jesus."

"I refusc to believe she'd betray us, though. I know Magdalene is still in love with Him, but she's more afraid of betraying me."

"It's your decision. If you want, I can order her imprisoned with the others. What do you think?"

"That sounds like the right thing. Arrest her and lock her in the basement with the others."

Adolf signaled his agents, who accompanied

him into the office. They left and arrested Magdalene, placing her in a cell with the rest of the prisoners.

Murmurs spread throughout the basement complex. Everyone discussed the arrest and that Magdalene was a prisoner. Two of the prisoners down the hall from her cell spoke loudly.

"You know, Luke, I always told Jesus not to trust that prostitute. She influenced Him so He believed it was me, not John, who betrayed us."

"We all knew it was John," Luke said. "Jesus didn't believe us, and neither do you."

"Look at her with her holy face, the damn whore."

"We must be prepared, Judas. Something serious is happening."

"Send a message to the prisoners in the cells beside hers. She's nervous and distraught. She'll confess if we pressure her."

"That's a good idea. If we can find out what's been going on the last 2,000 years, we'll be better prepared. We've been in here that whole time, and Jesus doesn't care. He never visits us. I don't understand why we're in here."

Chapter VI

The message was passed among the prisoners until it reached the cell beside Magdalene's. They had to find out what was happening and why they were still in prison.

"This is a surprise," a prisoner in the next cell told Magdalene. "It seems things have changed for you, too. Want to talk about it?"

She began crying. A few minutes later, she calmed and spoke with Hafid, the nearest prisoner. She didn't know him well, but she read the book *The Greatest Salesman in the World,* which described the wisdom of Hafid and the exemplary human being he'd been on Earth. She felt safe with him, and he told her despite everything, he felt compassion for her. His intelligent manner soothed her. Her remorse was obvious. She'd been Peter's accomplice for 2,000 years, helping to imprison all of Jesus' innocent contributors.

"Why'd you join Peter," Hafid asked, "when you knew he changed, and his actions were contrary to Jesus' intentions? I assure you that Jesus doesn't know we've been here for two thousand years. Why'd Peter do it? He has kept us from working with the divine plan, which is the reason we lived honest lives on Earth, free of sin. Do you know why?"

She cried again.

"Tell me. Come clean."

The other prisoners listened intently and spoke softly among themselves, although only a few could overhear the conversation.

"It's clear something isn't going well," Hafid said. "Take advantage of that and tell me what happened with Peter and Jesus. Are they no longer the divine beings we met?"

"Tell them to forgive me," Magdalene said. Suddenly, she shouted, "Forgive me! I betrayed you! I let myself be blinded by greed and pleasure. Peter was kidnapped and has been held in the palace library in solitary confinement all this time. I betrayed you, and Herod took his place."

"Herod?" the other prisoners asked in shock.

"Yes. Herod has been pretending to be Peter all along. A group of his friends accompanies him. He has a plan to kill Jesus along with all of you...I mean, all of us. Lucifer is on Earth, planning a massacre that will happen simultaneously with the murder of Jesus and Mary."

"How could you betray us for all those people?" Hafid asked.

"I gave in to pleasure and his promise to make me his wife. He threatened me constantly, saying he would hurt me if I repented from being involved with them."

"Does Jesus know what's going on?"

"No. He thinks all is quiet and normal. Herod's agents always surround his office. I never had a chance to approach him alone. I tried today, but they caught me. Lucifer's behind it all. He brought Herod and Adolf here to carry out his project.

"Herod became king in Hell and managed to be admired by all there. I got involved with all this. That's the price of ambition. Lucifer wants to reign on Earth. All of Jesus' decrees are filed, and a contrary decree is sent to Earth instead."

"How could you be capable of such a betrayal?"

"I told you. He threatened me. They never let me be alone with Jesus. Whenever I went there, someone accompanied me to watch me."

"Why didn't you say anything to us?"

"Agents always accompanied me here, too. They feared my loyalty and would have killed me if I spoke."

"What's with all the nervousness today? It's been an intense evening."

"Someone on Earth is trying to communicate directly with Jesus. They fear he will tell Jesus what's really happening on Earth and expose everything."

"How could he communicate with Jesus?"

"Martians have been facilitating on Earth, using the technology we gave them long ago."

"As far as I know, that technology was exclusively for the Martians."

"Yes, but that memorandum never reached Mars. Herod sent a fake one that gave specific instructions to the Martians to make the technology available to Lucifer, so their faction can communicate among themselves and between Earth and here."

"How did the person who wants to communicate with Jesus acquire the technology?"

"I don't know."

One of Louis' agents on Earth shared a cell with Tony. He gave Tony all the codes required to reach the Heavenly Palace and Mary, Jesus' mother, with the intention of revealing Louis' plan. It was difficult in the beginning, but Tony convinced him it was the right thing to do. The agent would be able to repay Louis' betrayal when Louis imprisoned him after a failed attack on a military base controlled by Louis.

"That call could come in at any time," Magdalene said. "If it does, Herod, Adolf, and Louis will be exposed. All terrestrial life will change, and Louis and his people would be annihilated. I wish they would call soon. Louis is planning to eliminate all terrestrial life and blame Jesus. Then Louis will reign, and Jesus will be hated for generations."

Hafid wasted no time passing on the message until all the prisoners understood the situation and remained on alert.

CHAPTER SEVENTEEN

Tension rose all that day and night. Fear gripped Herod until he finally decided to call Louis and set their plans in motion immediately. Their objective was to kill Jesus, Mary, all the prisoners, and then all the inhabitants of Earth. Louis and his collaborators would be spared.

They discussed whether to kill Jesus immediately or wait until Louis finished with the inhabitants of Earth first. They finally concluded that Jesus and the prisoners should die first and began their preparations.

In the basement, Hafid tried to persuade Magdalene to convince the agents guarding them to warn Jesus. She slowly liked the idea.

"That's the only way to prevent everything that's going to happen," Hafid said, pointing at an agent. "Convince him."

"How?"

"You know how. You're beautiful and sensual."

Magdalene sighed, knowing it was the only way. She unbuttoned the first two buttons on her blouse and released her hair, then wet her lips with her tongue. Her lashes, still damp with tears, added to her appearance.

She called to one of the agents. When he came closer, she said, "I'm scared. I'm worried about what's happening. I was made a prisoner without any reason. You know I've been good to you, and I want you to help me. I'm so scared. Feel how my heart beats."

She placed his right hand to her chest but dropped it to her left breast. He immediately blushed when he touched her hard nipple. Magdalene was desired by all. She was sensual enough to attract Jesus long ago.

"Madam, you know I can't break my oath to protect Jesus."

"Precisely. If you don't help me, you won't protect Him. Have you ever wondered why Peter was made a prisoner along with all the others?"

"Yes, but I didn't want to know. I prefer to continue without understanding."

She knew she needed to act fast. Pretending disappointment, she moved away from the bars, sat on the bed, and lifted her right leg to expose her tiny white panties that barely covered her.

The agent was paralyzed with lust, and she pretended she didn't notice. He stared, unable to look away from her intimate parts. He held onto the heavy bars, frozen in place. She slowly walked back to him, rubbing her nipples against his hands.

"Please help me," she begged.

He sweated in the cold basement. He had often told the other agents how beautiful she was and what he'd do if he had her. "What do you want me to do, Lady?"

"Listen to me carefully." She pressed her lips against his cheek, pretending to talk in secret, while her wet lips rubbed his cheek.

He retreated quickly, ordering his subordinate to stay alert.

Magdalene remained motionless, her hands holding the bars, looking triumphantly at Hafid, who had discreetly listened to her conversation.

"You've begun the process of undoing your mistakes," he said softly.

"I'll do whatever He asks me. If he wants sex with me, I'll do it, but I don't want to."

Chapter VI

The agent approached the door to Jesus' office, still hearing Magdalene's message in his mind. *They'll kill you. Herod is here.*

When he neared the office, he trembled at the sight of Herod and his agents and worried that Magdalene had betrayed him, but that wasn't the case. Herod was there with Adolf discussing who to assign to the murder of Jesus and Mary. To the depths of their being, they feared harming the Holy Family and took advantage of the agent's presence to ask him to carry out the mission.

"Are my instructions clear?" Adolf asked.

"Yes, Sir. I'll kill Jesus immediately, then I'll find His mother and kill her, too."

"We'll wait for you in Herod's office."

The agent hesitated, then walked into Jesus' office. Trembling in fear, he said, "You...You...You're going to die. Herod is here. Magdalene asked me to tell You."

CHAPTER XVIII

On Earth, Louis was trying to carry out his part of the plan as soon as possible. The MECOSA was already being distributed by his partners, in an area not far from there, they were also preparing to cause the largest detonation in the history of mankind. Louise was ready to command them to press the button.

In the prison where Tony was the guard began his usual tour around the cells. Once he passed by Tony's cell, Tony took out a cell phone and began to register a series of alphanumeric codes. Those were the codes given to him by Louis' agent when he was there; in retaliation for what he believed was an unjust imprisonment.

The agent said, in the presence of Louis, that generation after generation would pass and no King nor Governor would equal the leadership of Jesus. Because of that, he became an enemy of Louis. He was later sentenced to prison for twenty years, following an unsuccessful attack against Louis' security base.

Jesus was still astonished after listening the message sent from Magdalene through the agent, when the phone rang. He hurried to answer the call. Herod had ordered the call be transferred which was done, because now there was no point stopping it. Jesus would soon be dead, that was what he thought. So why be worried about the call.

Things were now clearer for Jesus. While talking to Tony, he better understood the message from Magdalene and acted immediately.

He promoted the agent who had brought him the message.

"Very well. Top Agent, listen carefully," Jesus said.

"Sorry, Sir, but I'm not a top agent, just a simple agent at Your service."

"Starting right now, you're My top agent and will be responsible for Palace security. Bring Magdalene to me immediately."

The new top agent left for the basement and returned a few minutes later accompanied by Magdalene.

"Tell me what the hell is going on here," Jesus said. "What does it mean to have him tell me, 'They're going to kill you. Herod is here?'"

Magdalene knelt before Him. Tears covered her face in seconds. "Forgive me. It's my fault. It's all my fault. I let myself be carried away by greed."

"How is Herod here?"

"He has always been here. Do You remember when You forgave Judas after finding out it was really John who betrayed You? It was when You sent me to get Judas out of hell and bring him to the Palace."

"Yes, I remember."

"Once I was in Hell, I let myself be led by greed. The power of Herod was so great in Hell, he was admired by all! His fame made me feel attracted to him. I betrayed You, Jesus. I betrayed all of you. I brought him here.

"Louis is also responsible. He kept calling me, trying to conquer me. He's the one who's responsible for Herod being here today. He put a lot of pressure on me and forced me to bring him here."

"How is it possible he's been here incognito for so long?"

"He hasn't been here incognito. He's been

masquerading as Peter all this time."

"Are you telling me that all the decisions made by this Palace and the execution of My orders have been in Herod's hands, not Peter's?"

"Yes. Not only that, but all Your memorandums were also replaced by ones created by others. Yours were archived, and those written by the others were sent to Earth to order the opposite."

"How is it that no one in my management team said anything about this?"

"They've been held prisoner all this time. Herod locked them in the basement except for Peter, who's in the library. He was separated from thc others because of his leadership over them. Herod feared a rebellion."

"Who's accompanying Herod here? Don't tell me that he was able to control all this himself."

"He's not alone. Once you signed the decree ordering Judas' release from Hell, this became a regular practice. Each week, Herod forged one of Your decrees and sent to hell for one of his own people. That's how he formed his team.

Adolf's arrival has been especially helpful. Herod appointed him top agent. Since then, he's overseen all regular business in the Palace."

"Are you talking about Adolf Hitler?"

"I am, Jesus."

He was infuriated to learn that Hitler was giving orders in the Heavenly Palace. "I've been betrayed once again. However, this time, I won't play the submissive, powerless man I did so many years ago. You shall feel My anger and fury. I'll make full use of My power, as I've never done before."

"Top Agent," Jesus said, looking at the man. "Arrest Herod and his agents. Bring these here before taking them to a cell. Magdalene stays here."

He acknowledged the order with great pleasure. Taking some of the officers who were guarding Jesus' office, he went out to arrest Herod and his men. Knowing the relationship between Herod and Magdalene increased his satisfaction.

I will have a clear path, he thought, remembering her hard nipples and the beautiful butt she showed him while they talked in the basement.

He approached the office where Herod and Hitler waited so eagerly to learn that Jesus and Mary were dead. While he and his men walked, he gave orders that once he walked into Herod's office, his men should start shooting all the agents outside. He was glad Herod left an order for him to be allowed inside.

The moment the door opened, the new top agent began shooting. Herod fell first, then Adolf. Agents outside the office died in a hail of bullets fired by his officers. None had the chance to defend himself.

He checked several other doors in Herod's office to make sure no one was there, then he removed documents from Herod's desk and walked back to Jesus' office.

"Sir, I have to inform you that while executing the arrest, Herod died along with Adolf. His agents were killed, too. I didn't have a choice, Sir. They resisted arrest."

The truth was, the agent didn't feel Herod and his people deserved any more chances. They had already caused too much damage. In addition, he couldn't forgive Herod for beheading his close friend, John and for the way Adolf on Earth caused the Holocaust against Jesus' descendants.

"Oh?" Jesus asked. "Well done. Stay with me while Magdalene answers more questions."

He turned to her. "Explain something to me. I received a call a while ago from Earth. I can't believe what's really happening down there. How did the situation reach this point?"

"During recent years, your decrees haven't been sent to Earth. That meant Lucifer acquired great power and became the leader of most nations. Those that refuse to follow him are crushed. Herod told me that the plan was for Lucifer to become king of the universe. According to him, you would be hated by all future generations, and he would take Your place."

The top agent spoke up. "Sir, she's right. I found this report on Herod's desk. It contains a well-structured plan to be carried out soon, and it's signed by Lucifer. There's another report about someone named Tony, but I don't know the reason for this one."

Jesus, accepting both reports, quickly scanned the pages. In under ten minutes, he read both voluminous documents. Anger showed on his face. He stood from his chair and began pacing, stroking his long beard. He stretched the ends of his white robe as if making a drastic decision.

He had to act quickly. At least Louis wouldn't know about the death of Herod and his accomplices.

"This report is ambitious," Jesus said. "Lucifer hasn't changed at all."

He lifted the other report in his right hand. "This report is about Tony, who called a while ago." He thought for a moment and turned to the top agent. "Be sure to kill all of Herod's accomplices. Keep the women and children in prison. We'll decide what to do with them later."

"Not Magdalene, Sir?"

Jesus looked at her. "We'll decide what to do with her later. Maybe she should be sent to live in the building in front of the Palace. Keep her monitored."

The top agent left, followed by his men, and gave Magdalene to one of them to escort her to a place where she could be locked up, but not in the basement. He wanted her alone, where he could conquer her when no one saw.

As he walked down the hall, he requested reinforcements. Within minutes, he was joined by other agents. All knew that Adolf and Herod were dead. Their men weren't ready to fight without a cause, so all surrendered.

He felt no compassion for them. As Jesus ordered, he killed them all, even those on their knees. He arrested the women and children and transferred them to the basement.

Once there, he called Jesus and asked, "Sir, what should I do with the prisoners in the basement?"

"Free them all."

Excitement rushed throughout the basement. All the prisoners spoke highly of Magdalene.

"The truth is," Judas said, "that bitch has earned our forgiveness."

"Certainly," Hafid said. "She has enormous

powers of conviction, and a beautiful ass. She convinced the agent within minutes and made him betray his loyalty to Herod."

Many embraced once they were freed. Then came Peter, who was isolated in the library, accompanied by Paul, who ran up to him when he came out of the library door.

Paul stared at Hafid, who said, "I see you looking at me. You don't remember me?"

"How could I forget my good friend?" Paul asked. "I remember your teachings."

1. Today I begin a new life.
2. I will greet this day with love in my heart.
3. I will persist until I succeed.
4. I am nature's greatest miracle.
5. I will live this day as if it were my last.
6. Today I will be master of my emotions.

7. I will laugh at the world.
8. Today I will multiply my value a hundred fold.
9. I will act now.
10. Never will I pray for the material things of this world.

Hafid and Paul hugged. Hafid remembered to whom he gave his most-valuable treasure and placed his hands on Paul's cheeks to kiss on either side. He recalled the beautiful memory of being a cameleer with the hope of succeeding in life only to give his merchandise to the baby Jesus to keep him from getting cold in that cave.

CHAPTER NINETEEN

After the trial, Roanne reviewed all the research she believed appropriate without finding anything that would help her get at the truth.

Three years later, she received an anonymous phone call. "I want to talk to you. It's about Tony. I'll wait for you tomorrow on the second floor of the restaurant on 51st Street and 8th Avenue at 12:30 PM."

The line went dead.

Roanne hesitated, then decided to go, feeling concerned for Tony's safety. After all, the area was very crowded, and the restaurant would be, too.

She arrived on time feeling nervous.

"Mrs. Roberts, how are you?" a man asked. "I'm Andrew Tomback."

"I see you know my name."

"Yes, I do. Please have a seat. Thank you for taking my call."

"I wasn't sure if I should come here. Taking into consideration how hard I've been working on this case, well, here I am. Whatever needs to be done, I'm in."

"Then listen to me carefully. I'm a Christian person. As a good Christian, I must promote justice and ensure the welfare of others. I also swore to care and protect my family. However, I'm in a situation where promoting justice and ensuring the welfare of others would risk my family's protection."

Roanne listened without replying.

"I'm an assistant attorney from the Southern District of New York. As such, I represent the government of the United States of America against a group of young men accused of multiple crimes. When I reviewed one of the defendants, he offered to clarify all his crimes and to testify against his co-defendants in exchange for a substantially reduced sentence. He not only offered information about the crimes he was charged with, but he also clarified other crimes in which he and his co-conspirators participated.

"To my surprise, the death of young Miss Dole came up, the crime for which your client, Tony Parker, is in jail."

Roanne's eyes widened in surprise. She

almost spilled her cup of tea.

"It turns out those were the young men who stole the tires from that vehicle, not Tony. They were the ones who started the shooting, too. I have a complete confession, sworn and signed. My witnesses are my assistants and the boy's attorney.

"However, when I told my superiors, they weren't surprised. Instead, their response was cold, and they told me to focus only on my own case, because Miss Dole's case was closed. That's my problem. If I act, I'll lose my job. If I don't, I'll bury justice and perhaps Tony with it."

Roanne was silent, thinking how to reply. "I always knew he was innocent. That's why I never gave up on his case. What can we do to resolve this for the best?"

"That's why I called. Something came to mind. It seems rather silly, but it might actually be a good idea."

"Tell me."

"I have a meeting set up with my supervisor on Sunday at his home. Here is the address." He handed her a piece of paper. "I'll be out of his residence by six o'clock, and it'll be dark by then. All these documents will be in my briefcase, but don't worry. I have copies in my office."

Roanne didn't understand at first, then she looked into his eyes and got it. "I understand. At six o'clock, it'll be dark. Thanks for everything, Andrew."

"You're welcome. Good luck."

"Good-bye."

Roanne stood and left the restaurant. She had to take possession of those documents, but she didn't know how. She understood what Andrew meant. She would have to steal the documents. If he could, he would have given them to her, but she knew he had to protect himself.

"What should I do?" she asked softly, driving down the road. "What shall I do?"

Suddenly, she smiled, thinking of her old friends. She came from a poor neighborhood, El Barrio in New York City. She was the daughter of a Puerto Rican woman and an African American. In her neighborhood, she was loved by all, mostly because she earned it. She hung out with the boys, even if most of them were juvenile delinquents. They respected her, because, despite hanging out with them, she always studied hard and talked about interesting things. They called her the Fine Fruit. She had a sophisticated vocabulary. Though her way of dressing was provocative, she was always formal.

Many of those boys remained in El Barrio. She drove there and parked in front of a certain building. When she got out, she called to a lady who was leaning out of her apartment window.

"Does the Fat Boy still live here?" she asked.

"Yeah. Who's looking for him?"

"Tell him it's Roanne."

"My God! You look like an executive." The woman suddenly recognized her, and Roanne knew her, too.

"Hey, Fat Boy!" the woman shouted. "The Fine Fruit's looking for you."

Roanne and the woman exchanged a smile.

"He's coming," the woman said.

Gordo walked out and stared. "My God, you look beautiful! You look like a high-class lady in that dress. You look really good, Mami."

Roanne wore an off-white suit with white blouse unbuttoned at the top to give a brief glimpse of her breasts. She wore high-heeled shoes and a black belt to match.

"What's up, Gordo?" she asked.

"Everything's cool. What are you doin' here? I haven't seen you in a long time."

"You know, Coño. I'm always working."

"So what?"

"I need you."

"Whatever you need, Mami."

When she started explaining, he was surprised.

"My God. I thought you did really good as a lawyer. What? You need money or something?"

She explained the rest of it, and he calmed down.

"OK," he said. "Now I understand. I don't even have to carry a gun. I like that. When is it?"

"Sunday at six. I'll pick you up at five. Is that OK?"

"Cool. How are your husband and kids?"

"The asshole left me. He told me I was a workaholic."

Chapter VI

"Please, Mami, marry me."

"Look, you bastard, you weigh too much. You'd crush me in bed."

"Bring the kids to see me someday. You know they'd be in good hands."

"I will."

She picked up Gordo at 5:00, as agreed. He stared down her blouse when she stepped out of the car for him to drive. He was silent, as if something bothered him, then suddenly stopped the car.

"Wait," he said. "I'll be right back."

"Where are you going?"

"I'm coming." He dashed into a clothing store and bought a pair of sports pants and sweater of the same color. He also bought gray sneakers to go with them and a blue sweater. He returned to the car and tossed the clothes on Roanne's legs.

"This is large," she complained. "They won't fit you."

"They aren't for me. They're for you. Don't think they're free. I need my money back."

"For me? Why?"

"Have you ever seen a thief dressed like you?"

She smiled. "Where can I change clothes? It's too late to go back."

"What do you mean? Change here."

"Here?"

"Yes, here."

She froze with indecision, as the fat man looked at her.

"What's wrong? Change your clothes, Babe," he said.

"I don't wear panties or a bra."

"Coño, much better, *pa mi.* I'll see your pussy."

Roanne smiled. "Look away. Don't look at me, you bastard, OK?"

She removed her shoes and lowered her pants carefully, revealing her beautiful butt. She checked to see if he was watching. She pulled on the sweat pants and gray sneakers, then removed her white blouse. Her nipples showed how cold it was in New York, as she pulled on the blue sweater.

Chapter VI

"I saw you looking, Asshole," she said.

"Not at you. I was looking at your pussy."

"*Cabrón.*"

Andrew left his boss' apartment at six o'clock in an exclusive area of lower Manhattan. The fat boy approached at a run, his right hand in his shirt to make Andrew believe he had a weapon.

"Give me the briefcase or die," Gordo said.

Andrew handed it over.

Gordo ran toward the car, and Roanne started the engine, accelerating the moment Gordo was in the passenger seat.

Andrew called 911, although he waited a few seconds for the red Mazda to leave the area. He told the patrol car it was a white car heading west, when in fact they drove east.

As they drove, Gordo said, "Man, I remember those times."

"You're being a good boy, right?"

"Yes. I have a wife and baby now."

"Keep it that way. Thanks, Gordo. I'll see

you soon."

"Good luck."

She gave him a quick kiss, and he stroked her hair to show the enormous affection he felt.

CHAPTER TWENTY

In the Heavenly Palace, Jesus remained on his throne with his top agent beside him, who returned after he killed all of Herod and Hitler's agents and imprisoned their wives and children.

"Sir, every moment is important," the top agent said. "We don't yet know how quickly Lucifer will carry out his plan."

Jesus listened, his expression showing his determination to act. His eyes transformed, as if being covered by clouds and turning stormy, just like the sky sometimes turned lighter just before a storm. A black cloud showed in his eyes, like the dark tunnel in which humans lived. He was ready to impose His punishment for disobedience.

"I warned them, but it seems they didn't believe," Jesus said. "I recommended them to be wise. My mandate was clear and precise in the memorandum I left. It's written in Chapter 6 1-8 in the Book of Wisdom in the Bible. It's so clear, only their own perversity prevented them from understanding.

"If all this happened here under my nose, can you imagine what it was like on Earth. I felt it in Tony's words. When I went into his mind and heart, I saw he was giving an accurate, honest account.

"By the way, Tony should be released immediately from prison. There's a report about him that will help. I have already created the conditions where it can happen.

"I am determined. This will be the day when they suffer the consequences of My wrath. I'm left with no other option, because they deliberately disobeyed My commands. They provoked My anger regardless of the consequences. They didn't follow My instructions and were influenced by Lucifer.

"They persecute the innocent without reason. Everything, however, has its time, and now is the time to eliminate the injustices on Earth. It's time to make the powerful of Earth understand their duty to the other citizens.

"This is the time to make them disappear, taking their injustices with them, so future generations will be protected. I will avenge. There will be no more executions of the innocent. Those who will come after will respect the laws and will use them to protect citizens.

"They have no respect for citizens' rights. They crush them like cockroaches. They sentence a boy for stealing a loaf of bread, but they never punish those who steal the boy's destiny. I blessed them with material wealth, but they spend it on wars against their own people.

"They give food to the hungry when they no longer have strength to eat. They arrive at the scene of a tragedy but do nothing to prevent it. They create laws to protect their citizens and turn those laws against them. They declare war on hunger and poverty but do nothing to actually win the war.

"They send people to get a job without making jobs available. They took my teachings from the schools, as if I were nobody. They just had to talk about me. It didn't matter under which doctrine they did it. They promote peace through violence. They discover cures for diseases and don't put them within reach of the sick. They promote democracy but impose the government's will on the people.

"As one of them said recently, they tail tens

of thousands of innocent people through a system of coercion. That is against My teachings and contrary to the ideals of those who founded their nation. They recognize people's rights and then refuse to respect them.

"This time, they'll understand. Lucifer will never be king of the universe. The generosity of those citizens will be reborn with his death.

"Only those who have shown extraordinary kindness and compassion for others will remain. The whole world will know what I'm capable of doing."

CHAPTER TWENTY-ONE

At the White Mansion, Louis celebrated with his cabinet. Sixteen bourgeois holding glasses of wine were ready for the final stage of Louis' ambitious plan. The MECOSA would be distributed that day, and the bomb was ready for detonation to produce a tsunami of the greatest magnitude that had ever been seen on Earth.

"From today, I'll be king of the universe!" Louis said. "I'd like to see Jesus' face when He finds out that those who followed Him don't exist anymore, and that He'll occupy my place in the minds of all future generations. Of course, that's if Herod doesn't kill him before He finds out."

"Bravo! Bravo!" the others shouted.

"My friends will be anxious."

"Just call them," someone said.

"No. I can't take the risk of the call being intercepted. They should be on the alert in case that guy eventually contacts Jesus."

Jesus remained in the Heavenly Palace with his top agent, preparing themselves. All His aides listened attentively to His instructions.

"I want it to be effective and coordinated," Jesus said. "I can already see the beginning of Lucifer's plan. He has begun distributing the MECOSA through the restaurants of his friends around the globe. That's the substance he described in his report to Adolf, which we now possess. He also plans to detonate a nitrogen bomb in the Pacific to start the biggest tsunami ever recorded. The bomb is ready to leave Louis' operations center in New Mexico, but I'll stop him. There will be some deaths, but I will eliminate the roots of Lucifer's plan."

"What do you wish us to do?" the top agent asked.

"Simon, call the Meteorology Center. Tell them to create the greatest storm ever seen on Earth. The rainbow won't appear until I order it.

"Luke, take this map. The red dots indicate where the lightning bolts must fall. At least five must strike each of those points. Give it to the Department of Energy."

"Sir, why such an intense storm?" the top agent asked. "That might injure our own people."

"No, Agent. This will save them. They

won't be able to leave their homes, and thus won't eat any of the MECOSA, which I imagine will be dispersed into the air.

"Once those points are destroyed, including the base in New Mexico, and the MECOSA is swept away by flooding, the storm will cease. I've already sent an angel to hinder any opportunity for the citizens to eat at fast-food restaurants."

The others followed His instructions immediately. In that region of Earth, the Meteorological Center warned of severe storms and flooding that would inexplicably occur in the next few hours. No one could explain how the clouds unexpectedly aligned to create the largest storm the nation had ever seen.

Thunder rolled, and lightning lit the sky across the globe. Huge thunderclaps boomed for several minutes. The country waited for the time the announcement could be made. The downpours were strong, as if all the fountains of the deep had broken, and the windows of Heaven opened. Winds ranged from 150-160 miles per hour, giving off all manner of sounds.

In every home, families watched it on TV.

No one had seen a storm like it before. Suddenly, all the stations became part of a national chain, where the announcement would impact everyone.

"We interrupt this programming to bring you unpleasant news. Five lightning bolts struck the white mansion that served as the residence of President Louis. He is presumed dead. Rumors have emerged that he was accompanied by his entire cabinet at the time of his death. We repeat...."

Other reports indicated that not far from the mansion, other large buildings were hit by strong lightning bolts. Preliminary reports said that at least 535 people died.

Another nearby installation was struck by a strong series of electric shocks, leaving a huge death toll. All the dead wore the uniforms of Louis' security detachment.

The shocking news made everyone in the nation stay with their TV sets, hoping to learn more. That followed Jesus' plan to keep them from being infected with the MECOSA.

Finally, the downpours stopped, and the rainbow arrived, as the sky cleared.

Chapter VI

Many newspapers had headlines with Louis' image sitting in a chair in his office, the bodies of sixteen other people around him.

Other pages had pictures of some of the 535 who died in an adjacent building to the White House. The dead bodies all sat in executive chairs, and the occupants wore suits and ties as if still in the throes of a long argument.

In another building not far away, a severe electric shock killed nine who were incinerated in the same room. The nation's citizens were shocked. It happened so fast. A few hours earlier, they feared a flood. Suddenly, the day turned clear and sunny, without any sign of rain.

Othcr news reached the national press. The lightning destroyed one of the city of Miami's convention centers. A conference was just beginning when the entire building collapsed after a huge explosion. No one could determine a cause for the death of so many members of the federal courts.

Electrical discharges also destroyed 215 other buildings throughout the country, killing a total of 16,025 people. It looked as if someone selected the blast areas very carefully.

The media were very busy that morning. Another 666 deaths were reported in separate incidents attributed to the storm's force. Medical experts, however, had another theory. They said the 666 died from some kind of blood freezing that required a unique combination of chemicals, but it was too early to determine the exact composition.

While more people were admitted to hospitals with symptoms of the virus, the media argued it could become a pandemic. Audiences asked questions of several experts, with the answers broadcast over the airwaves.

An elderly woman called CNN from her hospital bed. She said she'd been infected with the virus, and, like her, many others would die soon.

"All those who will die from this virus had something in common," she said. "They ate at fast-food restaurants. They'll die from food that has been infected by a deadly substance. It will always linger in those restaurants."

The old woman hung up. Members of the

media rushed to her hospital room, hoping to photograph her and ask questions. Unfortunately, the old woman disappeared mysteriously from her room.

A bedridden girl who was in the same room where the call took place said an elderly woman with white hair had been in the room with her. However, the hospital administration denied it, saying the hospital was reserved for children. No one had registered any elderly women there. Even though the call clearly originated from within the hospital, that bed had been empty for weeks.

The girl, who awaited surgery to regain her sight after a car accident, got up from her bed and ran to her mother when she entered the room. "I can see, Mom! She told me I could see you!"

The media gave extensive coverage to what the old woman said. Many citizens were frightened enough to stop patronizing fast-food restaurants, so those organizations quickly went bankrupt.

In His Heavenly Palace, Jesus looked

satisfied. His assistants watched, staring, as they perceived His eternal goodness, His compassion for others, and His courage in defending His cause.

CHAPTER TWENTY-TWO

In prison, Tony awoke exalted when a guard knocked on his door. He checked his watch and saw it was 7:30 AM. Looking at the Bible still beside his bed, he saw it was open to the Book of Wisdom 6:1-8.

"You have a visitor," the guard said.

Tony pulled on his khaki uniform and barely had time to brush his teeth and urinate before he left. The officer waited and took him to a visiting room to speak with Roanne. They were glad to see each other.

"How are you?" Roanne asked.

"Surprised by your visit. Don't tell me I was in a dream of yours, and you decided to visit me because of it."

"No, you weren't in my dreams. I wanted to tell you, though, that we have a court hearing at two o'clock this afternoon."

"A hearing?"

"Yes. Please forgive me for not telling you before. I didn't want to raise any false hopes. Now the chances are very good. It's possible you'll be released today."

"Are you serious?"

"I'd never play with something like this. Yes, I'm very serious. I have proof showing your innocence. I'll tell you all the details later. I just wanted to inform you before going to court."

Tony remembered his dream, and tears came to his eyes, as he gently touched her hand. "I always knew this day would come."

"I have to go, but I'll see you in court. Everything is arranged. I tried to communicate with your wife, but a gentleman answered the phone and then hung up."

"I know."

"I'm sorry."

Once in court, Tony had a very strange feeling that he realized was fear. He was back in a courtroom, but that time, everything was quite simple.

The prosecutor and the judge agreed to release him. It took only fifteen minutes.

His long agony was over. Tony almost couldn't believe it. The prosecutor, who previously accused him of being so aggressive, even smiled and raised his right thumb. Tony, not knowing what to say, stared back without any gesture.

The judge withdrew all charges against Tony. Tony was eager to know what was happening in the outside world. Roanne walked with him and gave him a full account.

He felt nostalgic when thinking about his family. They went to a restaurant near the courthouse. Once there, Roanne continued her story. He couldn't eat anything she ordered for him, as tears rolled down his cheeks.

"Doesn't it seem incredible how everything turned out?" she asked.

"Yes, but tell me, how'd you convince the prosecutor to agree so easily?"

"It was amazingly simple. Once I had the proof, I asked to see him in his office, and he agreed. At first, he wanted to know how I got the documents that proved your innocence. I replied that all that mattered was I had them, and they were real. I asked him what he would prefer—meet me in court or have me take the story to CNN? He was furious at the start, but then he agreed to go to court.

"That was three months ago. I have the impression he was concerned about his future, because he was guilty of concealing material evidence of a crime. He wanted to run for New York State senator. With this, he'll think twice about it. Just to get you out of there, I promised that if he cooperated, I'd take it into account."

"What should we do now?"

"That's your decision. You didn't make any promises, did you?"

Both smiled.

She watched, as Tony became deep in thought.

"What's wrong?" she asked.

"You won't believe it, but there are things in life we strive to call coincidences, but I think they have another name. Believe me."

"What's that?"

"Miracles."

"Why?"

"If I told you what I dreamed last night, you'd understand, but forget it. It was just a dream."

"OK. What's the one thing you want most of all to do now?"

"You mean other than seeing my children?"

"Of course."

He smiled. "I can't tell you. I'm sorry."

"But if you tell me, maybe I can help."

"I don't think so. This one is impossible."

"Come on, tell me. Let me know what it is."

"What's I'd like most right now is a night of pleasure."

"Ah, that! That's far easier than what I've done for you so far."

He stared, surprised to see she wasn't joking. "I think we'd better leave."

They looked silently into each other's eyes, then they walked out.

Once in her car, he added, "You know what? I want to dedicate myself to your.... Is the offer you made me still available?"

"Certainly."

"We'll go after each one, and they'll pay for this."

CONCLUSION

There are stages in people's lives where they choose to lose faith. One common reason is a lack of answers for their questions. The reality is, even though people seek answers, they never find them.

In my first novel, I tried to find answers even if they existed only in the imagination. This novel is fiction, but I feel convinced that in some parts of the world, mainly in the United States, some people will read this novel and say, "This happened to me," or, "I know someone who went through something like this."

When one's faith is tested, he might feel that the only reasonable explanation for such outrageous injustice on earth is that God no longer controls Heaven. That's a common feeling, and I've had it, too. However, it's just a feeling. God is still in control.

Through my imagination writing this novel, I found answers to my questions with the sole purpose of keeping my faith.

I prefer to imagine it happened and not to lose hope.

I prefer to imagine it happened, to continue believing in Him.

I prefer to imagine it happened, to take care of my health.

I prefer to imagine it happened, to follow my purpose.

I prefer to imagine He acted so, to continue believing in His promises.

I prefer to imagine it happened, to continue believing in justice.

I prefer to imagine it happened, to know that there is evil.

I prefer to imagine it happened, to believe that He listened to me.

I prefer to imagine it happened, to accept that I lost her.

I prefer to imagine it happened, to continue believing in love.

I prefer to imagine it happened, to believe I can talk to Him.

I prefer to imagine it happened, to believe in repentance.

I prefer to imagine it happened, to know that there is betrayal.

I prefer to imagine it happened, to know that there is a Lucifer.

Chapter VI

DEDICATION

If *I* listed all the reasons why I dedicated this novel to them, the dedication would be longer than the book itself.

So, I'll just say, to Issa, Roissita, and Robertico, with love.

Roberto S. Beras

ABOUT THE AUTHOR

Robert S. Beras was born in San Pedro de Macoris, a small town in the eastern part of the Dominican Republic. He is the third child of a single mother of five children, an incredibly hard-working woman who is always generous with her children. He grew up in a humble environment, and even though his mother didn't make enough money, he never considered himself poor, because he always had roof, food, education, and clean clothes.

He has a passionate love for sports since childhood, especially baseball and Ping Pong, two disciplines where he earned medals in local games.

He attended primary and secondary education in public schools and private schools, where he always admired the dedication and efforts of his teachers. However, one school and teacher left deep traces in him—his home, which he considers his best school; and his mother, who perhaps unwittingly was the best teacher for him.

He studied accounting at the Universidad Central del Este in the Dominican Republic. After a young marriage, he was eager to move forward and emigrated to the U.S.

It was a life of sacrifices but also happiness, blessed and filled with new experiences. He worked long hours each week, but even so, took time to study English at the Berlitz School of Languages in America, and he entered Hostos Community College in the Bronx, New York. He continued his studies in computer programming and computer systems at La Guardia Community College in Long Island City, New York.

He participated in a specialty program at Fordham University, a prestigious university in the city of New York.

He entered the business world, reached executive positions, and became a director of his own business. It was there that his odyssey began and where he currently lives. Although the Supreme Court of the United States held that the alleged act based on which the government keeps him in prison isn't a crime, Roberto has remained in prison. He struggles daily to get the court to declare his innocence, but the court denies it on a legal technicality. Meanwhile, he stays focused on this difficult time doing worthy things.

He served as a volunteer for twelve years in the church and remains attached to his Catholic faith. He currently practices law as a jailhouse lawyer after obtaining a certificate in paralegal studies with a specialization in civil litigation from Ashworth University, where he graduated with honors and an associate of science applied to accounting.

With this, his first novel, Robert has ventured into the world of writing.

www.ingramcontent.com/pod-product-compliance
Lightning Source LLC
Chambersburg PA
CBHW070609300426
44113CB00010B/1464
* 9 7 8 0 9 9 8 8 6 7 1 0 6 *